DAVID C. COOK VBS
Cosmic City™
EXPLORE THE AWESOME WONDER OF GOD

Outer Limits Upper Elementary Guide

Cosmic City™ VBS
OUTER LIMITS UPPER ELEMENTARY GUIDE
Published by David C. Cook
4050 Lee Vance View
Colorado Springs, CO 80918 U.S.A.

David C. Cook Distribution Canada
55 Woodslee Avenue, Paris, Ontario, Canada N3L 3E5

David C. Cook U.K., Kingsway Communications
Eastbourne, East Sussex BN23 6NT, England

David C. Cook and the graphic circle C logo
are registered trademarks of Cook Communications Ministries.

©2007 David C. Cook. All rights reserved.
Except for brief excerpts for review purposes, no part of this book may be
reproduced or used in any form without written permission from the publisher.

ISBN 978-1-4347-9953-1

Cover Design: BMB Design
Interior Design: Sandy Flewelling (TrueBlue Design)
Art: Aline Heiser, Mark Stay, Russell Tate
Photographs: © Brad Armstrong Photography
Space Photographs: © Corbis

All Scripture quotations, unless otherwise stated, are from THE HOLY BIBLE, NEW
INTERNATIONAL VERSION. Copyright © 1973, 1978, 1984 by International Bible Society.
Used by permission of Zondervan Publishing House. All rights reserved.

Thanks to our gifted development team!
Rebekah Atkinson, Jeff Barnes, Mary Grace Becker, Cheryl Crews, Leigh Davidson, Caroline Ferdinandsen, Diane Gardner, Nancy Haskins, Jodi Hoch, Kate Holburn, Sharron Jackson, Janet Lee, Marcia Lioy, Douglas Mauss, Scot McDonald, Susan Miller, Kevin Mullins, Carol Pitts, Jan Pendergrass, Karen Pickering, Loreta Riddle, Gail Rohlfing, Christina Schofield, Sheila Seifert, Judi Tippie, Kelli Trujillo, and Dawn Renee Weary.

Printed in China

David C Cook
transforming lives together

Welcome to Cosmic City's Outer Limits! No mission could be more exciting—or vital—than drawing your upper elementary students closer to the Lord. We're pleased you've chosen to join us on this journey. You're embarking on an out-of-this-world adventure that brings the wonder of God to life.

During David C. Cook's 2008 upper elementary Vacation Bible School, your Space Voyagers will venture into the farthest reaches of the known universe. As they explore some of the most exciting and extreme outer limits of creation, they will, most importantly, experience the awesome wonder of God.

Students start each day by **exploring** the wonder of God. First off is an opening assembly featuring the first half of the daily skit and a missions project update. Then Space Voyagers transition into a time of worship and praise, followed by an interactive Bible story and discussion. Before moving on to the next phase of their *Outer Limits* experience, students learn the day's Key Bible Verse and **Live It!** statement.

Next, it's off on an **expedition** to space's most dangerous outer limits, from the surface of the sun to the edge of a black hole. While there, Space Voyagers will discover all sorts of amazing facts that showcase the mysterious wonder of God's vast creation, followed by an extreme game. Space Voyagers then slow down a bit for a spacey snack.

Finally, Space Voyagers get a chance to **experience** God's wonder by working on a craft that reinforces the verse and taking part in an activity that equips them to **Live It!** in their daily lives. Students finish the day at a closing assembly where they view the conclusion of the day's skit.

We've given you everything you need to make this incredible week easy to plan and manage. This guide provides easy suggestions and materials to transform your *Outer Limits* site into each day's far-out space destination. Every activity students participate in is founded on biblical teaching, ensuring that this space adventure will change lives.

Everything you need to get started is waiting for you in the pages ahead and in this kit. So get ready for a week that will change lives and prepare for lift-off to the *Outer Limits*—where kids, and their leaders, explore the awesome wonder of God … and never return the same.

—The David C. Cook VBS Development Team

Table of Contents

Introduction 4

Outer Limits Debriefing: Week Overview 8

Characteristics of Preteens 10

Preparing for *Outer Limits* 12

Voyage Essentials: Master Supply List 19

Cosmic Caring: Special Learners 20

Abridged Travel Manual: Bible Story Summaries 22

Mission Command: Leading a Student to Christ 26

Voyage 1: *God's Wondrous Creation* 29

Voyage 2: *Desert Wonder* 41

Voyage 3: *Healing Wonder* 53

Voyage 4: *Water Wonder* 63

Voyage 5: *The Wonder of God Brought Down to Earth* 75

Skit Scripts 89

End Notes 112

Cosmic City™: Outer Limits
God's Wonder—See It, Know It, Live It.

What is Outer Limits?

Outer Limits is David C. Cook's brand-new VBS experience for fourth and fifth graders. Over five exhilarating days, your students will take a virtual journey through space. As they discover the wonders of the galaxy and explore fascinating stories from the Bible, they'll learn about a God who is both cosmically great and closely personal.

This innovative five-day experience takes the exciting *Cosmic City™* theme to the next level, engaging students with age-appropriate activities and discussions. Students at this age are unique in almost every way; they're no longer little children, not yet teenagers. For this special group of preteens, we've created custom-fit encounters with God … encounters that will transform their lives.

Launch Farther!
Check out the *Cosmic City™ Director's Guide* and the CD-ROM for some great promotional materials! Posters, bulletin inserts, and postcards are available specifically for *Outer Limits*. They're a great way to get out the word on this preschool program.

How is Outer Limits designed?

Outer Limits is different from the elementary *Cosmic City™* VBS. Each day, you will guide students through three adventure points: **Exploration, Expedition,** and **Experience**.

EXPLORATION
Students begin their day with an *Opening Assembly* that includes the first part of the day's *Skit*. They then spend time in *Worship*, and move on to interactively explore the *Bible story*, *Key Verse,* and *Live It!*

EXPEDITION
Students *Journey to the Outer Limits*, then connect that thrilling space destination to a creative *Game* and *Snack*.

EXPERIENCE
Students engage in an age-appropriate *Craft*, which reinforces the Key Verse, make a personal connection to their lives in the *Live it! Activity*, then end with *Closing Assembly* and the second part of the day's *Skit*.

You may also choose to have your sixth graders participate in *Outer Limits*, since we've designed all of the activities and discussions to meet the unique needs of preteens ranging from fourth to sixth grade.

Each student learns in a different way, so each adventure engages a unique learning style. Activities involving creative movement, quiet contemplation, verbal expression, logic and reasoning, hands-on challenges, and other learning styles will help students grow closer to God in the ways that work best for them.

The types of activities in *Outer Limits* vary as well, including writing, art, games, role-play, worship, crafts, and more. Whether an idea is high-energy or contemplative, serious or hilarious, it is guaranteed to be significant to each student's heart, mind, and soul.

Outer Limits is designed so it can run concurrently or at a different time than *Cosmic City*™ VBS.

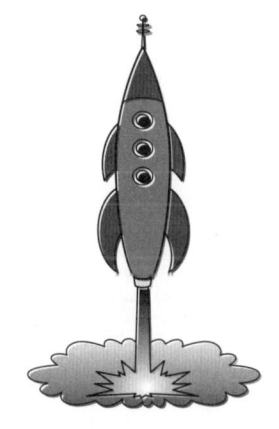

Student Books

The student books—otherwise known as *Mission Logs*—are central to the *Outer Limits* experience. This is where students will find discussion questions, trivia and images of their destination, and vital elements for many activities. In addition, each *Mission Log* includes a take-home page that gives students real-life challenges for applying what they learn each day. They'll also find creative ideas and discussion prompts to involve the entire family in each faith expedition. These innovative and colorful student papers guide students into a deeper exploration of God's amazing character, and a more intimate relationship with Jesus. You can order a *Mission Log* for each student at www.cookvbs.com.

Mission Project

SHARE THE WONDER: THERE— BIBLES FOR BRAZIL

Share the Wonder is this year's David C. Cook mission project. Money raised will provide the gospel to impoverished children in Brazil. These children will discover the wonder of God as they receive the gospels in their own language. The books they will receive are beautifully illustrated, which is particularly meaningful since literacy rates in many areas of Brazil are extremely low. As an added bonus, a generous donor will match the gift you send dollar for dollar, which means that for every dollar your students raise, two *Life of Christ* Bibles will be provided for children in Brazil.

Participating in the project is easy. Simply collect the money (see **Quick Tip!**) and send it to Cook Communications Ministries International. A poster is included on the *Cosmic City*™ CD-ROM along with a bulletin insert in the *Director's Guide*, so you can invite your whole congregation to join in! We've even included stories each day of *Outer Limits* that highlight how much these gospels mean to the people receiving them. All stories are true and taken directly from the report of a missionary in the area. Tell these stories to the students each day and watch God work as your Space Voyagers Share the Wonder.

For more details, ask your VBS Director or see complete information on pages 46–47 of the *Cosmic City*™ *Director's Guide*. This information can also be found in a colorful poster presentation and as a bulletin insert on the *Cosmic City*™ CD-ROM. And don't miss the Portuguese *Life of Christ* book sample in your VBS starter kit!

QUICK TIP!
Collect the money each day in a glass jar, fishbowl, or even a cardboard box fashioned to look like a space shuttle. Then print out the rocket ship art provided on the CD-ROM. To show kids the difference they're making, place two copies of the rocket ship art on the wall for every dollar donated. Each ship represents one book!

Launch Farther!

SHARE THE WONDER: HERE—
Impact Your Community

This year's mission project, Share the Wonder, offers an option that helps children further understand what reaching out to others really means. This optional addition to the world mission project provides kids with an opportunity to make a difference in their local area. Explain to students that God wants us to help people in our own neighborhoods too. Then pick one of the following projects to complete during the week:

School Supply Drive: Have children provide new school supplies for children in need. Gather everything from paper and binders to pencils and rulers. (Consider distributing a list of supplies to avoid over-duplication.) Remember that containers such as backpacks, book bags, or even boxes are needed. Your church can give these school supplies away to families within your congregation or broader community if needs are already known, or they can be given to a counselor at a local school who will give them away. Track how many children are being cared for as supplies come in. Since this project requires a little time investment from parents, you may wish to mention this project ahead of time when announcing VBS to your church. Above all, be sensitive to the privacy of any families in your church who may need these items.

Adopt-a-grandparent: Create a "quilt" for the residents of a nursing home. It can be made from individual sheets of paper decorated with encouraging messages and pictures from the children. (Be sure each child signs his or her quilt square!) The papers are then hung together in a quilt pattern at a local nursing home with a simple border created from sheets of brightly colored construction paper. If you know people who are skilled at sewing, you can also make a real quilt with fabric squares and bright fabric pens. Include a note that tells the residents who the quilt is from, or even send along a video message from the students in which they present the quilt and sing some of the songs they've learned during VBS.

Caring for your own neighborhood: Look around your church's neighborhood to find ways students can minister to people in their own community. Your pastor or a resident of the neighborhood might know of some needs that could be met. Be creative and help open your students' eyes to the needs right in front of them!

6 COSMIC CITY™ VBS Outer Limits Upper Elementary Guide

Outer Limits Terms List

Here's a list of frequently-used terms that will help you better navigate this resource:

* **Contemplating the Journey** – Optional idea that will slow down the energy (and noise) for a few minutes and guide students to meet with God in quiet meditation. In the midst of their often busy and noisy lives, this is a valuable chance for students to experience God in an intimate and personal way.

* **Worship Blastoff** – Ideas for your worship time with students that include using the *Cosmic City™ Music and Promo* DVD and *Praise Songs* CD, fun motions, praise through singing and scripture, live music, and both well-known and original worship songs.

* **Launch Farther!** – Tips to make the experience more impactful and memorable. If you have the time and resources, these ideas will help you take an activity to the next level.

* **Mission Briefing** – Large-group time.

* **Quick Tip!** – Brief, helpful ideas to ensure each part of the week goes more smoothly and effectively.

* **Shuttle Teams** – Small groups of students for activities.

* **Mission Logs** – Alternate name for Student Books.

* **Space Voyagers** – Alternate name for students.

* **Stellar!** – What students shout when they've finished a challenge or come to an idea.

* **Tour Stops** – Various stations students visit throughout the day (Exploration, Expedition, Experience).

* **Voyage** – Alternate name for each day: Voyage 1, 2, 3, 4, and 5.

Outer Limits Debriefing (Week Overview)

	LIVE IT!	BIBLE CONTENT — Bible Story	BIBLE CONTENT — Key Verse	EXPLORATION
Voyage 1	God's wondrous creativity has no limits! I can experience him everywhere.	God's Wondrous Creation (Gen. 1:1—2:4; Ps. 136:1–9, 25–26)	**Psalm 90:2** Before the mountains were born or you brought forth the earth and the world, from everlasting to everlasting you are God.	Experience a skit, worship, and creatively explore the Bible story through visual snapshots.
Voyage 2	God's wondrous trustworthiness has no limits! I can be secure.	God Provided Manna, Quail, and Water for the Israelites (Exod. 16:1–17, 31–36; 17:1–6)	**Isaiah 58:11** The LORD will guide you always; he will satisfy your needs.	Experience a skit, worship, and creatively explore the Bible story through different viewpoints.
Voyage 3	God's wondrous power has no limits! I can put my faith in him.	Jesus Heals a Paralyzed Man (Luke 5:17–26)	**Psalm 77:14** You are the God who performs miracles; you display your power among the peoples.	Experience a skit, worship, and explore the Bible story through "backward" storytelling.
Voyage 4	God's wondrous plan has no limits! I can live boldly.	Jesus Walks on Water (Matt. 14:22–33)	**Mark 10:27** All things are possible with God.	Experience a skit, worship, and explore the Bible story by defining key words.
Voyage 5	God's wondrous grace has no limits! I can spread his good news to others.	Jesus' Resurrection (John 19:1–6, 16–18; 20:1–8)	**Philippians 3:10** I want to know Christ and the power of his resurrection.	Experience a skit, worship, and explore the Bible story by drawing storyboards.

COSMIC CITY™ VBS Outer Limits Upper Elementary Guide

EXPEDITION	SNACK	EXPERIENCE	CRAFT
Journey to the Rings of Saturn with a game, and explore God's creativity.	Eat *Pizza Planets* or *Meteor Munch*	Worship God at creative stations, then gather for a closing assembly that features the conclusion of the day's skit.	Make *Creation Bracelets*.
Journey to the surface of Mars with a game and explore God's trustworthiness.	Eat *Modern Manna* or *Planet Pops*	Creatively consider what's needed to be spiritually secure; then gather for a closing assembly that features the conclusion of the day's skit.	Make *Duct Tape Survival Kits*.
Journey to the Sun with a game and explore God's power.	Eat *Sun Burst* or *Pudding Pop Walk*	Commit to having faith in God and reflecting his light and power; then gather for a closing assembly that features the conclusion of the day's skit.	Make *Sonshine Reflectors*.
Journey to a Comet's Tail through a game and explore God's plan.	Eat *Peach Boat* or *Boats-a-float*	Determine how to follow Jesus boldly; then gather for a closing assembly that features the conclusion of the day's skit. **QUICK TIP!** For Day 4, you'll use the craft for your game time. You'll notice that your Space Voyagers will create the craft before playing the game on this day.	Make *Flying Comets*.
Journey to a black hole through a game and explore God's grace.	Eat *Berry Blastoff* or *Resurrection Butterflies*	Commit to spreading the good news to others; then gather for a closing assembly that features the conclusion of the day's skit.	Make *Butterfly Backpack Danglers*. Alternate craft: *One-of-a-Kind Keychains*

COSMIC CITY™ VBS Outer Limits Upper Elementary Guide

Characteristics of Preteens
Why are these students special?

We understand that every preteen has unique needs, desires, and ways of learning. Yet we also recognize that there are certain characteristics common to many upper elementary students, generally between the ages of nine and twelve. We've created *Outer Limits* to reflect that understanding.

Here are a few characteristics of preteens that will give you extra insight into your students' journey through *Outer Limits*. Following each characteristic is a practical application you can use as you minister to these students:

★ **Generally concrete, but becoming more abstract.** Up to this point, they've not grasped abstract concepts—and some still may not—but they're increasingly able to link the concrete to the non-concrete and make the logical connection.

Application: It's okay to use metaphor and subtlety in your teaching, letting students discover spiritual meaning on their own. But make sure you're there for students who need the final dots connected to fully grasp the point.

★ **Full of energy and curiosity.**

Application: Give them experiences that involve energy and spark curiosity.

★ **Variety of emotional and physical maturity.** No two students are alike—which is what makes ministering to this age level so exciting, and often challenging.

Application: Discard any one-size-fits-all theories. At the end of each day, note every participant's level of emotional and physical maturity to help you interact more meaningfully with each student.

★ **Experiencing lots of changes.** Repeat: *lots and lots* of changes. Their bodies, their friendships, their thought patterns, and their emotions are all changing at a rapid pace.

Application: Exercise patience. Your preteens may feel as if they're traveling at light speed through an asteroid field, and they need you to display grace and understanding.

★ **Desperately want love and acceptance.**

Application: This doesn't mean you should accept or love everything they *do*. Actually, challenging students to think or act differently (about God, others, and themselves) may be the best way to love them. For a refresher course on true love and acceptance, read about how Jesus challenged people with love. (See Matthew, Mark, Luke, and John.) It's the best encouragement out there!

★ **Growing up in communication overload.** They have access to technology, information, and entertainment like no generation before them.

Application: Although it may vary from student to student, acknowledge their familiarity with things like iPods, computers, video games, and cell phones. Be relevant to their world—what they know, have, and experience.

★ **Not protected from loss, pain, and lifestyle change.** Most of your students have been impacted by death, whether of a family member or a pet. Furthermore, many have experienced divorce or have friends with divorced parents. It's also possible that a number of your preteens have moved or changed schools.

Application: Learn your students' stories. Get to know where they're coming from, what makes them sad, excited, and scared. Your ministry will be more effective.

★ **Moving toward independence.** Preteens are beginning to express themselves individually, developing their own identities. However, they still retain a strong need to fit into a group.

Application: Whenever you can, recognize their individuality—the way they make decisions, express themselves, and respond to God and others. The respect you show will affirm them and keep them growing toward healthy independence.

★ **Becoming more articulate.**

Application: Offer lots of opportunities for your students to practice their verbal skills, especially their thoughts about God. The more comfortable they get at clearly expressing themselves, the more they'll articulate their faith to friends.

★ **Thinking more about the present than the future, and more about themselves than others.** This is natural for a preteen; it doesn't mean they're extraordinarily selfish or small-minded.

Application: Keep your eyes open for ways to challenge students to reach beyond themselves and practice empathy, compassion, and foresight. (Taking the time every day to focus on the "Here and There" aspects of the *Cosmic City*™ VBS mission project is a great way to do this!)

★ **Functioning well as a group.** Your students enjoy being part of a group—and have a great capacity for working together to solve problems, learn, and encourage one another.

Application: Take advantage of the benefits a group brings; introduce activities that require cooperation, and be amazed at what they accomplish together.

★ **Craving your guidance and authority.**

Application: No, really. The structure and boundaries you set make students feel safe, which in turn encourages them to offer more emotionally, mentally, and spiritually.

Preparing for Outer Limits

Prayer

You're probably already praying that *Outer Limits* will be an effective, life-changing week for your students. Involve your team in prayer meetings on a regular basis before the program starts, and then every day both before and after the day's experience. Refer to the list of participants, praying for each student by name.

Ask your church congregation to pray for your students, as well. You may mention your specific requests during services, or put together a flyer asking for prayer support. Invite the congregation to join you in asking God that *Outer Limits* runs smoothly, blesses the families of the students, holds real spiritual significance to each participant, and is truly out-of-this-world.

Volunteers

Outer Limits will, in great part, go as well as you and the other leaders guide the program. So it's essential that you involve the best people in your team. You must value the specific gifts and skills each volunteer brings, and not be satisfied with just finding a warm body to fill a spot. (Read on for what makes an excellent volunteer.)

How you use volunteers is entirely up to you. Consider dividing up the many roles and tasks among volunteers: registration, shopping, financials, daily set-up, and clean-up. Ask volunteers what they're interested in doing, and try to assign them to a role that fits their personality and spiritual gifts.

You may choose to have a different volunteer lead each portion of the program: Exploration, Expedition, and Experience. If you have a volunteer who's skilled with food or crafts, ask this person to head up the snack or craft activity. The more energetic volunteers would be perfect for the game activity. Dividing up these tasks is simple: just separate each Exploration, Expedition, and Experience section by gently tearing along the perforation. Then distribute each to the person in charge.

RECRUITING VOLUNTEERS

Recruit volunteers with different strengths and weaknesses. They'll combine to form a well-rounded team of leaders who'll be balanced and equipped in every area. For instance, recruit some detail-oriented volunteers (who may not be able to see the big picture), and some visionaries (who may be terrible with details). This way, you're covered no matter what the need is.

Only you know how many volunteers you need. However, a good rule of thumb is to aim for about one leader for every five students. If you have more, congratulations! If you have fewer, don't panic. We're sure your wonderful volunteers will guarantee a terrific experience for each student.

CHARACTERISTICS OF WORLD-CLASS VOLUNTEERS

As you seek and find the right helpers for Outer Limits, look for these marks of a great volunteer:

- ★ **Flexible.** (No, not physically, although that's not a bad thing either!) Using humor and improvisation when the unexpected happens.
- ★ **Innovative.** Taking every opportunity to turn a "normal" moment into a "heavenly" discovery for students.
- ★ **Teachable.** Always desiring to learn from God as students learn from them—humble, ready to do things differently if it'll be more effective.
- ★ **Loving.** Giving students what they need: guidance, kindness, and the best listening skills this side of Jupiter.
- ★ **Fun.** Enjoying kids of this age will enhance the students' experience.

TEENAGE HELPERS

Involve youth group members in your VBS ministry; the experience will strengthen their leadership skills and their own faith. Give teenagers jobs they're interested in and well-suited for. For instance, acting in the skits is a perfect task for youth. You'll also want at least one or two teen helpers, called Teen Guides, available to circulate throughout the room to help students with everything from crafts and games to role-plays and reading Scripture. Be sure to equip your teen helpers with needed tips and advice before they take on any role.

TRAINING

Once you have a leadership team in place, plan to meet at least once a week, beginning about a month before the program starts. At these meetings, spend time getting to know one another and bonding over your shared passion for preteens. Go over the essentials: your goals for each day (and each section of each day); your expectations for what the leaders will do and how they'll do it; and your plans for particular tasks and assignments (such as set-up and food preparation).

In these regular meetings, you might also carry out the specific training you think is necessary. For instance, share discipline techniques or prepare for answering the "tough questions" that may arise during the week. Talking in pairs or role-playing scenarios will likely help with this training. You might distribute materials on theology or the background of the featured Bible passages. You can also give volunteers information on leading students to know Christ (see pp. 26–28).

Ask your team for suggestions on how best to prepare for the program; their questions and ideas will help you focus your training on what's most important.

The more you meet, the more you'll like and trust one another. This camaraderie will be valuable during VBS, so do all you can to build your team "spirit" beforehand. What about renting a movie about space or watching one at a local I-MAX theater? At the end, hold an impromptu trivia game and see who can come up with the most space facts from the film. Or, what about just getting together for coffee, games, and conversation? This relaxed time will prompt people to open up, share about themselves, and laugh together. Each time you meet, spend time praying. And don't forget to dream big together! Get excited about what God will do in your students' lives and hearts during *Outer Limits*.

Promotion

Try any or all of these ideas to publicize *Outer Limits*:

★ Make announcements to the congregation during church services and distribute "spacey" postcards, bulletin inserts, or flyers. See the *Cosmic City*™ CD-ROM for these items.

★ Pique interest with a fun skit during your church service (you might even "preview" one of the morning skits from *Outer Limits*).

★ Put up promotional posters around your church and community. Grocery stores, libraries, and coffee shops are great places to catch people's attention. Work with volunteers (teens would be great here) to create colorful designs that feature space destinations such as the Sun, the Moon, a comet, and so on. Include the dates, times, and contact information on the poster, as well as a catchy slogan such as "Journey to the *Outer Limits* and Discover the Center of the Universe." You can also download the *Outer Limits* poster from the Cosmic City™ CD-ROM and customize it with your church's specific information.

★ If running your preschool *Blast Off!*, elementary *Cosmic City*™, and upper elementary *Outer Limits* programs concurrently, promote them together. Each has been created to coordinate with each other in theme, Bible content, and life application, so highlight them as a whole. You can download a poster from the *Cosmic City*™ CD-ROM that promotes all three programs.

Set-Up

PLANNING YOUR SPACE

Look at each day's activities, plan which options you'll choose, and determine the kind of space you'll need. You might use one general area such as a youth room. Or, you might set up in several rooms throughout the church—outside for the games, sanctuary for the opening assembly and worship rally, and children's Sunday school rooms for the crafts. You might have small groups go into different rooms for discussion time. If running *Outer Limits* concurrently with *Cosmic City*™ VBS, plan carefully to provide ample space for both programs.

Keep in mind that some activities, particularly the games, may require more space than it originally seems. It's a good idea to plan accordingly.

DECORATING

Here are some ways to make this adventure really feel like the "outer limits" of the universe. Feel free to do whatever fits your time, space, and budget. Remember, a little effort will go a long way in setting the right atmosphere.

★ Paint one or more black sheets (or other fabric) with many white dots, apply glow-in-the-dark stars, and put them up on a wall or the ceiling of your room.

★ Stick glow-in-the-dark stars and planets on the ceiling or any other surface. Sets of glow-in-the-dark space objects featuring each day's Key Verse can be purchased for each individual student. Extra sets can be ordered and used in decorating. Check out www.cookvbs.com.

★ Color several hard foam balls of different sizes and hang them from the ceiling using string and pushpins.

★ Buy inflatable space shuttles, planets, and stars from a local party store. Scatter them around your space.

★ For a cheaper alternative, construct space shuttles by attaching construction paper fins and cones (the nose) to two-liter plastic bottles. Hang these homemade rockets from the ceiling, or set them in the middle of snack or craft tables.

★ Spray paint large balls (such as already-inflated beach balls) in vivid colors and set them on the floor as rolling "planets."

★ For a sci-fi look, make control panels with buttons and knobs glued to aluminum-foil-wrapped cardboard. Or, you might just bring in computer keyboards or laptops. (Just be sure to keep these protected. It might be a good idea to take them home each night.)

★ Borrow a congregation member's telescope; set it in a corner of the room, pointing up. (Again, be very careful with this and anything else you borrow. Don't leave them in the room unless you can lock the door overnight.)

★ Replace light bulbs with colored bulbs such as yellow (for the sun), blue, green, orange, or red. Black lights can also be used to create a unique, spacey effect.

★ Make a few changes to your area every day to match each individual destination and transport students (and their imaginations) to the "Outer Limits" of the universe. Here are some simple ideas to bring each voyage alive:

Voyage 1: The Rings of Saturn. Make circles the theme of your space. Hang hula hoops from the ceiling. Using colorful butcher paper, create a large paper image of Saturn; be sure to create the rings out of a different color from the planet itself. Create large circles on the floor using masking tape or colored electrical tape.

Voyage 2: Mars. Think red. Red butcher paper on the walls, red Styrofoam balls hanging from the ceiling, even red light bulbs in a few lights (giving the whole area a reddish glow).

Voyage 3: The Sun. This is a great day to brighten up your space. Create a huge wall-sized sun using yellow butcher paper or poster board. Hang smaller cardboard suns from the ceiling, cover the floor with a large yellow tarp (just be sure not to play games on it; you don't want students slipping during their visit to the sun), and gather extra lamps for additional bright lighting in your area.

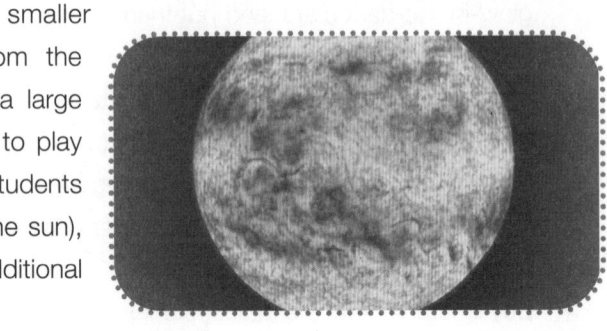

Voyage 4: A Comet's Tail. Try creating a sense of motion and speed in your space. Create a large moving comet for the wall by cutting a large circle out of butcher paper or poster board and attaching long strands of crêpe paper streamers to one end. Use streamers liberally throughout your area, hanging them straight down from the ceiling.

Voyage 5: A Black Hole. Save the best for last and wow your students with a space that resembles the eerie environment of the universe's deepest known corners. Cover the walls with black butcher paper and replace a few of the lights with black light bulbs. You'll want to turn on the regular lights for much of the program, such as games and crafts. Then use the black lights to set the atmosphere as students arrive.

Three-Hour Schedule

	Min.	Suggested Time
Exploration *(including Worship, Contemplating the Journey)*	75	9:00-10:15 a.m.
Expedition	45	10:15-11:00 a.m.
Experience	60	11:00-noon

Two-Hour Schedule

	Min.	Suggested Time
Exploration *(omit Worship, Contemplating the Journey)*	45	9:00-9:45 a.m.
Expedition	30	9:45-10:15 a.m.
Experience	45	10:15-11:00 a.m.

Schedule *Outer Limits* can take place concurrently with *Cosmic City*™ or at a different time. If you choose to run both programs simultaneously, you may opt to have snack time together. This is dependent on your space and other concerns; for instance, in a smaller church facility, it may be easier to do snacks separately to avoid overcrowding an area.

Outer Limits can take three hours each day, or you can modify the program to fill a two-hour time slot. Here's a basic outline for each option. Follow whichever works best for you (or create another plan to fit the time you have).

Leader Tips

To guarantee a truly "stellar" week:

- **Ask, don't tell.** Hesitate in suggesting what students should think or believe. Instead, focus on asking great, open-ended questions, and let students come up with answers on their own. They'll mean more to them this way.
- **Ask great questions.** The most effective questions are always specific, d personal, and meaningful—and sometimes controversial or difficult. The generic, impersonal, obvious questions (anything answered with "yes," "no," or "Jesus") don't pull out the most valuable insights.
- **Don't avoid the tough stuff.** When hurt or fears arise in discussion, look students in the eyes and let them know you'll face it with them. These are often the most powerful God-moments. Then be sure to follow up with students; be true to your word.
- **Choose your battles.** Some students may misbehave, but don't be too quick or zealous in disciplining. Of course, you want to ensure that everyone has the opportunity to learn without distractions, so balance calm guidance with grace.
- **Adapt and improvise.** The activities and questions in this resource are scripted, but you don't have to follow them as written. Use the framework as a starting point, and adapt the content to fit the needs of your students.
- **Pray, pray, pray.**

Expectations of Leaders

Here's a planning checklist that'll help you make sure that every base is covered and every detail is taken care of throughout the entire *Outer Limits* process.

FOUR MONTHS BEFORE

- ☐ Pray for the leaders and children who'll be part of *Outer Limits*.
- ☐ Read through the entire program.
- ☐ Create an *Outer Limits* planning committee.
- ☐ Schedule *Outer Limits* on your church's calendar (in conjunction with VBS).
- ☐ Establish a working budget for *Outer Limits*.

THREE MONTHS BEFORE

- ☐ Hold regular planning meetings. Assign jobs to *Outer Limits* committee members.
- ☐ Recruit someone to oversee set-up of all of *Outer Limits* and gather a team to help.
- ☐ Recruit leaders and helpers, including actors for opening and closing skits.
- ☑ Recruit people to pray, provide transportation, and provide follow-up.

COSMIC CITY™ VBS Outer Limits Upper Elementary Guide

Expectations of Leaders, continued

- [ ] Order and/or create all the publicity pieces (bulletin inserts, posters, postcards, etc.) you'll need as you promote *Outer Limits*. (You can order Publicity Packs at www.cookvbs.com.)

TWO MONTHS BEFORE
- [ ] Assign leaders for individual responsibilities.
- [ ] Make photocopies of activities delegated to multiple leaders.
- [ ] Make photocopies of skit scripts for all actors. (see pp. 89–111)
- [ ] Have the leaders put together a team to help decorate and plan. Remind each leader to order any needed supplies and decorations from www.cookvbs.com immediately.
- [ ] Use resources on the *Cosmic City*™ CD-ROM to promote *Outer Limits* within your church (announcements, posters, etc.).
- [ ] Hold regular staff training sessions.

SIX WEEKS BEFORE
- [ ] Publicize *Outer Limits* to your community through posters, newspapers, and "community events" radio spots.
- [ ] Meet with your teams regularly.
- [ ] Make sure that leaders are preparing.
- [ ] Continue training for all VBS staff.

FOUR WEEKS BEFORE
- [ ] Announce *Outer Limits* in your church to create interest and enthusiasm.
- [ ] Begin a registration drive.
- [ ] Double-check all props, supplies, music, snacks, etc.
- [ ] Confirm that the actors are preparing.

ONE WEEK BEFORE
- [ ] Review the details with leaders and teams.
- [ ] Make signs to help the first day go smoothly.
- [ ] Prepare a checklist for each area of *Outer Limits* to make sure everything goes smoothly.

THE DAY BEFORE
- [ ] Set up *Outer Limits* Voyage 1 and make sure everything is ready for the first day!
- [ ] Pray with your *Outer Limits* staff.

DURING *OUTER LIMITS*
- [ ] Gather the supplies for the next day's Voyage.
- [ ] Set up the area for the next day's Voyage.
- [ ] Refresh the general supplies as needed.
- [ ] Review the next day's activities; make adjustments where necessary.
- [ ] Remind your leaders about tasks and assignments.
- [ ] Remind your actors to practice skits before each Voyage.
- [ ] Plan for the Closing Assembly celebration on the final day.
- [ ] Invite parents to the Closing Assembly celebration on the final day.

THE WEEK AFTER
- [ ] Clean.
- [ ] Return all borrowed items.
- [ ] Give away any extra food and supplies to families in need.
- [ ] Send thank-you notes to church leaders and volunteers.
- [ ] Thank students personally for taking the journey to the *Outer Limits*, and continue to ask how they're doing.
- [ ] Update the name and address list of leaders, helpers, and children for follow-up as well as for next year's program.

Voyage Essentials—Master Supply List

General Supplies
- [ ] *Mission Logs*
- [ ] CD player
- [ ] Computer (for accessing the *Cosmic City*™ CD-ROM to download *Outer Limits* promotional tools)
- [ ] Bibles
- [ ] Pens
- [ ] Markers
- [ ] Paper (lined, unlined, and construction)
- [ ] Scissors
- [ ] Paper towels
- [ ] Facial tissue
- [ ] First-aid kit
- [ ] Tape (transparent and masking)
- [ ] Pushpins
- [ ] Sticky tack
- [ ] Ribbon
- [ ] String
- [ ] Small paper or plastic cups
- [ ] Index cards
- [ ] Glue
- [ ] Sequins
- [ ] Glitter
- [ ] Clay or play dough
- [ ] Whiteboard or large poster

Voyage 1 Supplies
- [ ] 7' of suede cord per student
- [ ] 7 plastic beads (6x9 mm) per child (one of each color: yellow, blue, green, orange, red, brown, and white)
- [ ] Sewing scissors (at least one for every three students)
- [ ] Tape
- [ ] Sample of completed craft
- [ ] Tape measures or measuring tapes (at least one for every three students)
- [ ] Paints
- [ ] 3-5 paintbrushes
- [ ] 3-5 sheets of praise music
- [ ] 3-5 pieces of blank sheet music, pencils
- [ ] Musical instruments (harmonica, recorder, acoustic guitar, etc.)
- [ ] 20 toothpicks
- [ ] Streamers
- [ ] Several small foam balls

Voyage 2 Supplies
- [ ] Water
- [ ] Tray
- [ ] Sheet
- [ ] Small everyday items such as:
  - [ ] Small umbrella
  - [ ] Stocking hat
  - [ ] Sunglasses
  - [ ] Winter gloves or mittens
  - [ ] Wool socks
  - [ ] Boots
  - [ ] Rope
  - [ ] Energy or granola bar
  - [ ] Paper towels
  - [ ] Resealable bag
  - [ ] Hard, round fruit-flavored candy
  - [ ] Adhesive bandage
  - [ ] Rubber band
  - [ ] Small candle
  - [ ] Doctor's mask
  - [ ] Pack of gum
  - [ ] Pocket Bible

- [ ] Compass
- [ ] 12.5' of duct tape per student
- [ ] Sewing scissors (at least 1 for every 3 students)
- [ ] Colored plastic tape
- [ ] Sample of completed craft
- [ ] Rulers (one per student)
- [ ] Cotton balls
- [ ] Paper clips
- [ ] Star stickers
- [ ] Sandpaper
- [ ] Pebbles
- [ ] Batteries
- [ ] Erasers
- [ ] Toothpicks

Voyage 3 Supplies
- [ ] Round mirrors, 2" in diameter (one per student)
- [ ] Blue, black, yellow, orange, and red craft foam (2 mm thick)
- [ ] Sample of completed craft
- [ ] Scissors (one pair per student)
- [ ] Rubber cement (one bottle for every three to five students)
- [ ] Magnet tape
- [ ] Ruler (for prep only)
- [ ] Hardback books (1 per student, to help craft remain flat while glue dries) (optional)

Voyage 4 Supplies
- [ ] Dictionary
- [ ] Small cup seeds or plastic pellets for each student
- [ ] Blindfolds for each student
- [ ] Ripstop nylon fabric (1/2 yard for every three students)
- [ ] Dried beans or peas (1/2 cup per student)
- [ ] Snack-sized plastic zip seal bag

- [ ] Sewing scissors (one pair per student)
- [ ] Measuring tape (for leader only)
- [ ] Rulers
- [ ] Markers (one per student)
- [ ] 1/2 cup measuring cup (at least one for every five students)
- [ ] Yarn or sturdy string (approx. 12" per student)
- [ ] 3 hula hoops (optional)

Voyage 5 Supplies
- [ ] Various colors of felt (e.g. white, green, pink, purple, red, black, orange) (approx. one 8.5" x 11" piece for every two students)
- [ ] Photocopies of the *Butterfly Backpack Dangler* pattern found on page 86 of this Leader's Guide (one copy of pattern per student)
- [ ] 6 mm googly eyes (two eyes per student)
- [ ] Small ball chains (to use for attaching to backpack) (one per student)
- [ ] Yarn (approx. 6" per student)
- [ ] Rulers
- [ ] Scissors
- [ ] Single hole punch
- [ ] Felt glue
- [ ] Pencils
- [ ] (optional) Glitter glue and/or puff paint
- [ ] (optional) Small gift bags and tissue paper
- [ ] Sample of completed craft
- [ ] 8" x 11" tag board (or corkboard) for every student
- [ ] 2-3 family-friendly magazines for every student (should include interesting images, not just text). (Check your local library or thrift store for free or low-cost magazines.)

Cosmic Caring
Special Learners

Launch Farther!
During a training or planning meeting, take a few minutes to talk about special learners you expect will attend *Cosmic City*™. Pray for them as a team, and share insights about what motivates or encourages the special learners.

QUICK TIP!
Children with special needs have unique styles of learning, but so do gifted and advanced learners. Keep in mind that some children may appear bored or even become disruptive when they master a concept or activity more quickly than the others. Engage these advanced learners by giving them opportunities to help their classmates or to create challenging additions to the activity.

Some kids can't. They really can't. Can't keep their feet still. Can't hurry up and get in line. Can't choose a snack plate more quickly. Can't sit in that chair for just a few more minutes. Can't listen to your voice and not hear the conversation happening on the other side of the room divider. Can't predict what will happen next no matter how many clues you offer. Can't stop rocking back and forth on the chair. Can't leave the fidget toy on the counter by the door. Can't read the words in bold. Can't stop spinning around. They really can't.

Kellie didn't like Sunday school because it involved too much reading. And although she was a bright child, reading wasn't coming easily. Her teacher no longer suggested that the class go around the table taking turns reading. Instead, she asked for volunteers.

Aaron wondered why Jason didn't have to come to the table with the rest of the class during the Bible story. His teacher explained that Jason learned best when he was up and moving around. Aaron, who loved to sit still and read, seemed puzzled at first. But when the Bible story was over and the teacher asked review questions, Jason knew all the answers. He'd heard every word. This led to a discussion with all the children about their various learning styles. A few weeks later, when a substitute teacher was having trouble coaxing Jason to the table, Aaron said, "That's all right. He learns when he's moving around. Just ask him any question!"

It's a Wide Spectrum

Kids learn in all sorts of ways—through words, music, movement, art, introspection, and so on. *Outer Limits* offers a range of learning activities that will touch kids in all these areas. But some kids will still need an extra dose of understanding because their development differs from other kids their age. They may simply need some extra time and encouragement, or they may have an identified disability that's mental, physical, or behavioral in nature. Attention deficit disorder, autism, Asperger's syndrome, Down syndrome, sensory integration disorder, obsessive-compulsive disorder, impulse control issues, social anxiety—kids walk through the door with a wide spectrum of challenges that we can't always see.

If you suspect you have a "special learner"—a child who seems to be developing outside the typical range—start by taking stock of what the child can or can't do. When the disability is physical, limitations are generally easier to recognize. If Frankie is in a wheelchair, you wouldn't think that he's able to get out of the chair to play the relay game with the rest of the class. Instead, you're likely to adapt the game so that Frankie can participate.

When disabilities or special circumstances aren't physical, avoid the temptation to think that the child just needs to try harder or listen to instructions better. Don't insist that Kellie really can read or that Taylor really can sit still and stop pushing buttons any more than you would expect Frankie to get out of his wheelchair.

Order in Chaos

Accepting special learners in your class doesn't mean giving in to chaos. All kids need structure and predictability. Use these suggestions to make special learners comfortable and to encourage appropriate participation as much as possible.

1. Adapt the way everyone does the activity. Make adjustments that include the special learner and still accomplish the goal of the activity. For example, if an activity calls for children to pass a squishy ball around the circle to the beat of the music, but you know Miranda will want to hold on to it, give everyone a ball made of wadded paper. Have each child pass his wad from one hand to the other, still to the beat of the music.

2. Arrange for extra help. Take advantage of Cosmic City's teen Guides. A child like Zack may need someone to be his buddy with gentle reminders of appropriate behavior. Sometimes just the presence of another adult or teen in the group helps all the kids stay within the right parameters.

3. Allow for variety. Not everyone has to do everything the same way. If Lynette wants to color her craft on the floor while everyone else paints at a table, so what? You're after participation and learning, not a battle for dominance.

4. Adopt new habits. Give warnings about transitions, clarify instructions, set supplies out ahead of time, touch a shoulder and smile, or make a point to speak a word of encouragement to a struggling child. Teaching children isn't as much about getting through the material as it is making connections that keep you in touch with what they're learning.

5. Adjust your attitude. Let's face it—some kids can be frustrating. You may even find yourself secretly hoping rambunctious Travis doesn't come tomorrow. But remember the attitude of Jesus, a sacrificial, humble servant who gave up the honor he deserved.

> **QUICK TIP!**
> Be so prepared on the first day that when kids arrive you can focus on them. Observe them and take note of insecurities or challenges you see so that you can help volunteers address them.

> **QUICK TIP!**
> If you're struggling to connect with a special learner, try turning your eyes inward. What is it about your own personality or background that may be contributing to difficult times?

Abridged Travel Manual—Bible Story Summaries

Day 1—God's Wondrous Creation

BIBLE STORY
God's Wondrous Creation (Gen. 1:1–2:4; Ps. 136:1–9, 25–26)

KEY VERSE
Before the mountains were born or you brought forth the earth and the world, from everlasting to everlasting you are God. (Ps. 90:2)

LIVE IT!
God's wondrous creativity has no limits! I can experience him everywhere.

A LITTLE BACKGROUND...

Today's Bible story explores the fantastic cosmic fireworks display that starts the Bible: God's creation of the world. And though the creation account is awesome on its own, it also points us to an important reality for all people of faith, both young and old alike. The apostle Paul explains in Romans 1:20, "Since the creation of the world God's invisible qualities—his eternal power and divine nature—have been clearly seen, being understood from what has been made."

We can see God's power through his amazing act of creation recorded in Genesis, and evidence of his reality and character by simply taking a look at the world he created.

Even a few moments spent contemplating God's amazing world inspires awe and wonder. Brilliant sunsets render us speechless. Sparkling stars on a quiet night trigger thoughts beyond earthly matters. The melodies of birds on a peaceful morning delight the soul. Even the thunder, lightning, and rhythmic sounds of a stormy night remind us how small we are in the grand scheme of life. More than anything, such occasions offer a brief glimpse of God's incredible majesty—a majesty praised by the elders in Revelation 4:11, "You are worthy, our Lord and God, to receive glory and honor and power, for you created all things, and by your will they were created and have their being."

God's incredible creation naturally fascinates and inspires children. By looking at the world they can begin to understand the God who made it and find their hearts worshipping him in response. Everything around them can become infused with great meaning and spiritual truth.

Today's exploration of the creation account points kids beyond simply *what* was created to *who* created it. As they participate today, children will discover important aspects of who God is: God is a creative artist, God is loving, God is powerful, God is personal, and God is *real*. And we can worship him!

Day 2—Desert Wonder

BIBLE STORY
God Provided Manna, Quail, and Water for the Israelites (Exod. 16:1–17, 31–36; 17:1–6)

KEY VERSE
The Lord will guide you always; he will satisfy your needs. (Isa. 58:11)

LIVE IT!
God's wondrous trustworthiness has no limits! I can be secure.

A LITTLE BACKGROUND...

Today's Bible story includes some serious complainers: a bunch of Israelites with bad attitudes wandering in the desert. It's easy to point a finger at them—but if we're honest, we have to admit that we often do the same thing! How many of us would be able to walk day after day through a blistering hot desert without complaining? Despite God's amazing provision in our lives, we often take for granted the truth that we can count on him, and instead fixate on all the parts of our lives that seem to be going wrong.

The events of Exodus 16 and 17 are set against the backdrop of some of the most amazing events in Old Testament history. God called Moses through a burning bush,

were freed, God parted the Red Sea, and through God's power the ferocious Egyptian army was annihilated. Talk about *awesome!* A display of power like this would be hard to forget; yet, sadly, the Israelites are quick to put this miraculous past behind them and find reasons not to trust God as they plod through the desert. It was only human for them to wonder, "If God loves us, then why is he making things so *hard* for us?"

Deuteronomy 8:3 tells us that God had a reason for the hunger and thirst he allowed the Israelites to experience during their desert wanderings: "He humbled you, causing you to hunger and then feeding you with manna ... to teach you that man does not live on bread alone but on every word that comes from the mouth of the Lord." God's purpose in providing manna, quail, and water was not just to meet the Israelites' physical needs—his intention was to show them that God himself is the perfect Provision they needed ... and *we* need. God is our manna—our bread. Jesus alluded to this same concept when he said, "I am the bread of life. He who comes to me will never go hungry, and he who believes in me will never be thirsty" (John 6:35).

It's in a relationship with God through faith in Jesus that our deepest hunger is fulfilled and our thirst is quenched. Through God's provision for the Israelites, kids can discover that God is trustworthy and they can count on him—not only for practical needs in their lives, but also as the true sustenance for their souls.

Day 3—Healing Wonder

A LITTLE BACKGROUND...

On the surface, the events of Luke 5:17–26 are stunningly spectacular. Some men, passionate about getting their friend to Jesus to be healed, don't let anything get in their way—not even a crowd of people or the roof of a house. They dig, cut, and rip their way through the roof in order to lower their paralyzed friend to the ground in front of Jesus. Then they wait in expectation. Will their hopes be answered? Will their friend be healed?

Jesus *does* heal their friend, and in quite a dramatic fashion. One minute, the man is motionless on a mat; the next, he's holding his mat under his arm and *walking* home praising God. Wow!

But there's a hidden thread in this story that's even more awe-inspiring than the physical healing that takes place. It's the profound healing power of Jesus' *words* that are the true miracle in this account. Jesus tells the paralytic, "Friend, your sins are forgiven."

Not only does Jesus provide outward, physical healing, but he also addresses the inner need of the paralytic and reveals himself as the true healer of humankind. Jesus uses this metaphor of physical healing to explain his reason for befriending sinners in Matthew 9:12, saying, "It is not the healthy who need a doctor, but the sick." Jesus, the Son of God, has the power to heal us of our deepest wound: our separation from God as a result of our sin.

Jesus' statement to the paralytic is profound not only for the forgiveness he offers, but also for the word "friend." It's in this kind first word Jesus speaks to the paralyzed man that we get a glimpse of the type of relationship God desires to have with us. Jesus

BIBLE STORY
Jesus Heals a Paralyzed Man
(Luke 5:17–26)

KEY VERSE
You are the God who performs miracles; you display your power among the peoples.
(Ps. 77:14)

LIVE IT!
God's wondrous power has no limits! I can put my faith in him.

calls the man not into a cold, distant religion with a remote, uncaring deity, but into an intimate *friendship* with the loving God who has forgiven him.

Today's lesson will allow children to share in the excitement of the men who brought their friend to Jesus and witnessed the miracle that happened that day. But beyond the events of the story, they'll learn the exciting truth that Jesus can heal *them* too. They can find this healing in the forgiveness of sins he offers and the friend relationship they can have with him through faith.

Day 4—Water Wonder

BIBLE STORY
Jesus Walks on Water
(Matt.14:22–33)

KEY VERSE
All things are possible with God.
(Mark 10:27)

LIVE IT!
God's wondrous plan has no limits! I can live boldly.

A LITTLE BACKGROUND…

It could be argued that all the disciples who were in the boat the night Matthew writes about in chapter 14 "trusted" Jesus. After all, many had made major sacrifices to become his follower, leaving their families and careers behind to travel from village to village. And they'd all just witnessed a fantastic miracle—Jesus had used five loaves of bread and two fish to feed over 5,000 people! Talk about a trust-booster!

That night, they *all* saw Jesus walking toward them on the water. But only *one* disciple, Peter, trusted Jesus enough to swing his leg over the side, place his foot on the water, and step out to Jesus.

For a moment, try to wipe away your familiarity with this story and see it with a fresh perspective. This was a real man doing something completely insane—hefting his body onto liquid H_2O. If you were there, would *you* have done that?

As we all know, the story doesn't end there. When Peter felt the rain pelting his face, heard the wind howling in his ears, saw the waves tossing about all around him, he was afraid and immediately began to sink. But Jesus saved Peter and challenged his faith, asking, "Why did you doubt?"

So, is the point of this story for us to berate Peter for his doubt and his lack of trust? Are we to hold Peter up as an example of a person with small faith, teaching kids to focus on Peter's failure?

Or instead, can we look at the story through a different lens? Step back from that scene of Jesus clutching Peter, pulling him up out of the waves, and focus in on the boat Peter left behind. That boat is full of Jesus-followers who *didn't* step out onto the water.

Clearly Peter still had growing to do, and the Gospels record many similar interactions between Jesus and Peter in which Jesus uses Peter's faults and failings to teach him about true faith (Matt. 16:21–28; 26:31–35, 69–75; John 21:15–19). But Peter's willingness to throw caution to the wind (literally) and step out onto the water is a powerful example we can use to show children what it means to truly trust Jesus.

We see another bold step from Peter just two chapters later, when he's the first disciple to courageously declare, "You are the Christ, the Son of the living God" (Matt. 16:16). Peter shows us that trusting Jesus isn't merely a mental assent or a casual relationship; it's not a safe faith that clings to the comfort and security of a familiar boat. It's a trust that steps out into the water—it's a risky, bold, whole-person response of complete commitment to Jesus. It's a trust that puts it all on the line in response to Jesus' call.

As you explore today's **Live It!** point with the kids, you can use the activities to help them see that they can trust Jesus to help them make it through the various challenging circumstances that come their way. But even more importantly, they can *trust* Jesus with their lives; they can believe in him with all their hearts, commit everything to him, and make him the Lord of their lives.

Day 5—The Wonder of God Brought Down to Earth

A LITTLE BACKGROUND...

Today's lesson introduces children to the meaning of the resurrection and the real reason it's so spectacular. It's not simply the miracle of a dead man coming back to life. It's the miracle of the defeat of sin and death, the miracle of forgiveness and eternity with God being offered to us undeserving humans. This isn't the ho-hum news or the so-so news—this is the *good* news! It's the best news ever, and it's worth celebrating.

This news is also worth *sharing*. When Jesus gave the Great Commission in Matthew 28:19–20, he didn't say, "And when you reach age eighteen, go and make disciples..." Jesus' kingdom includes its youngest citizens and his commission applies to them as well. Jesus commended the trusting, honest, open, and sincere faith of children (Matt. 18:3 and 19:14). And the truth of the matter is, kids can sometimes do an even *better* job than adults at sharing their faith! As they reach out to their friends and playmates by sharing Jesus with them or inviting them to church functions like Sunday school, a midweek program, or VBS, they have the ability to plant seeds of faith. Today, as Space Voyagers get a closer look at Mary, Peter, and John's excitement about telling others the good news, watch *them* get excited about their own mission. They too can share the "awesome news" about the best day ever seen on planet Earth.

BIBLE STORY
Jesus' Resurrection (John 19:1–6, 16–18; 20:1–8)

KEY VERSE
I want to know Christ and the power of his resurrection. (Phil. 3:10)

LIVE IT!
God's wondrous grace has no limits! I can spread his good news to others

Mission Command
Leading a Student to Christ

It's amazing how often adult Christians say that they first came to understand the unfolding of God's story when they were between six and twelve years old. These years are a key time for children to make personal decisions for Christ and to begin their faith journeys. *Outer Limits* may be the experience that makes a student think about expressing faith in Christ and receiving God's saving grace.

Keep in mind that no two young people are at the same point of spiritual preparedness. Many students aren't ready to trust in Christ even at the upper end of elementary school; others can be quite sincere in saying they want Jesus to be their Savior even as preschoolers. They're sensitive to their need for forgiveness and acceptance into God's family. Be open to the Holy Spirit's leading. Be available to answer questions, but let Space Voyagers decide when the time is right to receive Christ. Here are a few tips:

★ Be careful not to let your eagerness spur Space Voyagers to make a faith decision, since VBS is a time when our radar is eagerly seeking students who are ready to trust Christ for salvation. Students may pick up on what will make the teacher happy and perhaps say they want to make a decision when the truth is they don't yet understand what they're saying.

★ Look for opportunities to invite students to receive Christ individually, rather than just making group invitations. Kids are great conformists; they may respond to such an invitation just because everyone else is doing it. Encourage them to talk privately with you about questions regarding salvation and what Jesus wants to do in their lives, and then be sure you're available for these conversations.

★ Have the student tell you in his or her own words what he or she wants. If you feel the student understands the concept of salvation and is ready to receive Christ by faith, take a few minutes to pray with him or her. You and the student will want to talk with his or her parents about this decision. Parents who don't attend church may have questions about salvation, and this opens the door for you to witness to them and invite them to your church.

★ Remember your important ministry of follow-up. Pray for the student and encourage discipleship and Christian growth. Send a personal note—kids love to get mail addressed to them! Follow-up photo frames are also available at www.cookvbs.com.

Explaining Salvation

The following suggestions may be helpful as you explain the message of salvation. Help the student know the truths that are fundamental for all Christians. Make copies of the next page (page 28) and have them available to all your adult and teen volunteers. This page will help students follow these important steps and give them something to take home as a reminder of their decision.

Step 1: God loves us even though we sin (Romans 5:8). We must recognize that we deserve God's punishment, and his love is a free gift (Rom. 6:23).

Step 2: Even though God loves us, our sin separates us from him. But he wants to forgive us, and he will if we ask (1 John 1:9).

Step 3: Believing in Jesus and inviting him to lead your life is the way to accept God's forgiveness (Rom. 10:9–10). Jesus is God's perfect Son, and he died on a cross to take the consequences of our sin (John 3:16). Jesus didn't stay dead. God brought him back to life to prove he's stronger than our sin. Because Jesus died and rose again, God can forgive us.

Step 4: Once we ask for God's forgiveness, we can celebrate because we're sure he forgives us (1 John 1:9). Now we're part of God's family forever (John 1:12), and we want to learn as much about him as we can. Reading the Bible, praying, and worshipping are some ways we learn more about him (2 Pet. 3:18).

Step 5: When we have the good news of being in God's family (John 1:12), we want to tell others about it (Matt. 10:32; 28:19). Encourage children to express their decisions in their own words. Clarify any confusion.

During your conversation, you may want to share some additional verses with the student. The verses below might help. Read them from a Bible, not just the page. You don't have to use them all in every conversation; different verses may answer the questions of individual children.

★ John 1:12—"Yet to all who received him, to those who believed in his name, he gave the right to become children of God."

★ John 3:16—"For God so loved the world that he gave his one and only Son, that whoever believes in him shall not perish but have eternal life."

★ Romans 3:23—"For all have sinned and fall short of the glory of God."

★ Romans 5:8—"But God demonstrates his own love for us in this: While we were still sinners, Christ died for us."

★ Romans 6:23—"For the wages of sin is death, but the gift of God is eternal life in Christ Jesus our Lord."

★ Romans 10:9–10—"If you confess with your mouth, 'Jesus is Lord,' and believe in your heart that God raised him from the dead, you will be saved. For it is with your heart that you believe and are justified, and it is with your mouth that you confess and are saved."

★ 2 Corinthians 5:17—"Therefore, if anyone is in Christ, he is a new creation; the old has gone, the new has come!"

★ 1 John 5:11–12—"And this is the testimony: God has given us eternal life, and this life is in his Son. He who has the Son has life; he who does not have the Son of God does not have life."

Discovering Jesus as Your Savior

1. God loves us, but he does not like our sin. The Bible teaches that all people have sinned or disobeyed God (Rom. 3:23).
How have you sinned by disobeying God?

2. The Bible says that our sin separates us from God (Rom. 6:23). But God provides a way for us to be connected with him again so we can live with him forever. We need God's forgiveness.
Do you want to know how to be forgiven by God?

3. Jesus is God's perfect Son. Jesus died on a cross to take the consequences for our sins (John 3:16). Because Jesus died for us, God forgives our sins.
Do you believe that Jesus died on the cross to forgive you of your sins?

4. Jesus didn't stay dead. The Bible tells us that he rose from the dead and is alive today! So we can talk to him right now. If we believe that Jesus died on the cross to take the consequences for our sins (Rom. 10:9–10), we can ask God to forgive us. The Bible promises that if we ask God to forgive us, he will (1 John 1:9).
Would you like to ask God to forgive you for your sins?

5. Once we have asked Jesus to forgive us, our sins are forgiven. Jesus saves us from the result of our sins. When we trust Jesus as our Savior, we are part of God's family forever (1 John 5:11–12). Because we are part of his family, we are to live in ways that please God and do things that help us learn more about him (Col. 1:10).
What are some ways you can learn more about Jesus?

6. Now that you are forgiven and part of God's family (John 1:12), you will want to share your decision with others.
Who would you like to share your decision with?

28 COSMIC CITY™ VBS Outer Limits Upper Elementary Guide

© 2007 David C. Cook. Permission granted to reproduce for use in the *Cosmic City*™ VBS program only—not for resale.

God's Wondrous Creation

VOYAGE 1

BIBLE STORY
God's Wondrous Creation (Gen. 1:1—2:4; Ps. 136:1–9, 25–26)

KEY VERSE
Before the mountains were born or you brought forth the earth and the world, from everlasting to everlasting you are God. (Ps. 90:2)

LIVE IT!
God's wondrous creativity has no limits! I can experience him everywhere.

Exploration (1 hour, 15 minutes)

OPENING ASSEMBLY – 30 minutes

Outer Limits Leader welcomes students.

Hello, Space Voyagers. Welcome to *Outer Limits*! You're about to take the journey of your life, to places no one has ventured before. We're so excited you're on board as we launch into the outer reaches of the galaxy—and discover God's amazing wonders. Today we're going to explore our first cosmic destination. Let's get our engines fired-up with an out-of-this world drama…

Actors perform the skit for Voyage 1: Part 1. The script for today's skit can be found on pages 89–91 of this guide.

Outer Limits Tour Host or another adult volunteer introduces the daily mission project.

Share the Wonder: There—Bibles for Brazil

During each day's opening assembly, you will collect students' money for the *Cosmic City*™ VBS Mission Project and give an update. More detailed information on this year's project is given on page 5 of this guide. In the opening assembly section of each

COSMIC CITY™ VBS Outer Limits Upper Elementary Guide

QUICK TIP!

Additional *Cosmic City*™ VBS music CDs and DVDs can be purchased at www.cookvbs.com.

QUICK TIP!

During this announcement time, you can ask students to bring money each day for the mission project. You might also describe the take-home portion of the *Mission Logs*, called "Back to Earth," highlighting the activities families can experience together. Additionally, you may give important information for students with food allergies, and explain what to do in the case of an emergency (describe where the first-aid kit is, and so on).

QUICK TIP!

To help students get to know each other, lead them through this fun ice-breaker: Tell everyone that when you say **Go!**, you want them to find one other person with whom they share something in common (for instance a favorite color). Say **Go!** and wait until everyone's in a pair. Next time, pairs must find one other pair, and all four people must have something in common (for instance, favorite pizza topping). Say **Go!** and wait until everyone's in a group of four. Keep on like this until everyone's in one large group.

---

day, you will find a script that gives information about the project and real-life stories of people in Brazil whose lives have already been changed by receiving the Word of God through this project. Feel free to use the scripts word-for-word or as a launching point for sharing your own thoughts and information:

What do you think it would be like to want to know more about God, but not have even a little bit of the Bible to help you? It would be very difficult! There are lots of places in the world where it isn't as easy to get Bibles as it is here. Let me tell you about one of those places, in the country of Brazil—in an area called Pernambuco. The people who live there are very poor. It's hard for them to pay for even the food they need, so a Bible costs far too much for them. Plus, it's difficult to even find Bibles. Many want to know about Jesus from the pastors and missionaries there, but there are no Bibles for God's workers to give them.

This week, we're going to do something very special for the children in that part of Brazil. We're going to collect money to send them books with the part of the Bible that tells about Jesus! It's in their own language, Portuguese. *Hold up the sample book.* **These books are special in another way too. They are filled with pictures that tell the story as well.** *Open the book to show the illustrations.* **That's important because most of the children we're sending these to can't read very well. Starting tomorrow, bring in any change you'd like to give to help send the books to Brazil. Every dollar you bring will provide two books. I'm going to place one of these rockets on the wall for every book we're able to send.** *Hold up the rocket picture copied off the Cosmic City™ CD-ROM.* **We can help the children there learn about God like we are this week! It isn't as easy for them. So let's see how many we can send!**

Tour Host gives announcements. Include any specific additional information.

For the next couple of hours, we're going to guide you through lots of great experiences. You'll do some activities alone, some in small Shuttle Teams, and some as a large group—otherwise known as Mission Briefings. You don't need to bring anything on this journey except your curiosity, energy, and ideas. If you have a question or problem at any time, let one of the Tour Hosts know immediately. Please do your best to listen well, learn new things, and not take away from anyone else's adventure. And, most importantly, have fun!

Tour Director, Tour Host, or teen Guide prays:

Dear God, thank you for bringing everyone here. Be with us this week as we explore the outer limits of space, life, and faith. Teach us what you want us to know so we can love you and others better. In Jesus' name, amen.

Worship Blastoff

A leader plays the *Cosmic City*™ theme song. You can choose to play the *Cosmic City*™ *Music and Promo* DVD with guided motions, have students create their own movements to accompany the song, or do the following: **Get on your feet—it's time to sing our theme song. As you sing the verses, clap your hands. When the chorus comes, spin in a circle … and keep spinning!**

Rally *(optional)* – 15 minutes

If you choose this option, play the *Cosmic City*™ *Praise Songs* CD for portions of this time and have a live worship band lead other parts. You may want to have the songs displayed on a screen using PowerPoint slides or an overhead.

We have a wonderful God who deserves our worship. One way we worship God is through singing songs of praise. Prepare to worship God with your hearts and voices.

Song suggestions:
- ★ *From Everlasting to Everlasting* (Sarah Moore, *Cosmic City*™ VBS *Praise Songs* CD and *Cosmic City*™ VBS *Music and Promo* DVD)
- ★ *God of Power* (Phil Reynolds, *Cosmic City*™ VBS *Praise Songs* CD and *Cosmic City*™ VBS *Music and Promo* DVD)
- ★ *Holy Is the Lord* (Louie Giglio and Chris Tomlin)
- ★ *Forever* (Jesse Reeves and Chris Tomlin)
- ★ *He Is Exalted* (Twila Paris)

Read the following passages aloud in between songs, have a volunteer read the verses aloud, or say the Scripture together: Psalm 19 and Nehemiah 9:6.

**BIBLE STORY/KEY VERSE/LIVE IT! –
30 minutes**

Have students form Shuttle Teams of four to six. Assign one team Genesis 1:1–8, another team Genesis 1:9–18, another team Genesis 1:19—2:4, and the last team Psalm 136:1–9 and 25–26. Have team members open up to page 3 in their *Mission Logs* (Student Books), circle their section of Scripture at the top of the page, then read it together as a team.

When everyone has finished reading, explain the activity. **As you've probably noticed, this is a very descriptive, visual Bible story. So, we're going to explore it visually. With your Shuttle Team, I want**

QUICK TIP!

If your church's youth group has a worship band, this is a great opportunity to involve teen volunteers. And, although a full band can work well, a single pianist or guitarist will be simpler and just as effective.

QUICK TIP!

You'll need a CCLI (Christian Copyright Licensing International) license for each song you play and sing during your worship time. Make sure your church has this license, or go to www.ccli.org to obtain it for a reasonable fee.

Launch Farther!

You may choose to add a competitive component to *Outer Limits*. Here's how this option works: Today before the Bible story exploration, assign students to Shuttle Teams of five to ten (depending on the size of the entire group). These Shuttle Teams will stay the same through all the voyages; however, if you don't use the competition option, teams can change from day to day.

Throughout the program, there are directions for students to form groups of various sizes and types. For each of those activities, you may instead have students form these competition Shuttle Teams, and go forward with the activity as planned. Have each Shuttle Team come up with a cool, "spacey" name, and create a team poster during the Voyage 1 craft. Each day, teams can earn Voyager Points by any of the following: memorizing the day's Key Verse and the **Live It!**; cooperating while creating their poster and during other activities throughout the week; winning the day's game; applying the day's **Live It!** at home; and cleaning up after the day has ended.

Delegate to a Tour Host the responsibility of keeping track of Voyager Points. This involves checking in with Shuttle Teams for a morning report, Key Verse recitation, and generally keeping up with any activity in which students could earn points. You may choose to reward Shuttle Teams with prizes at each day's closing assembly or at the end of the week.

QUICK TIP!

If you have a large number of students, either form bigger Shuttle Teams or give each passage to more than one team. If you have a small number of students, assign two or three passages to each Shuttle Team.

Launch Farther!

Some of these questions, as well as a summary of the Bible story, can be found on page 3 of each Voyager's *Mission Log*. You may want to have students meet with a partner to read the summary, then discuss the questions. Or, you can even have each Space Voyager go through the questions in a self-guided exploration, writing answers along the way, then meet back with the large group to debrief.

you to express to the rest of us what your specific passage was about. Remember, no one else read your verses, so you have to be as descriptive as possible. When I tell you to, you'll represent your part of the story with a three-second moving snapshot—kind of like a brief video. You can use sound if you'd like, but it must all take three seconds or less. I'm going to give you a minute or two to plan out what you're going to do. To let me know when you're ready, I want everyone in your Shuttle Team to shout "Stellar!" at the same time. Just so you know, this'll be the catchphrase for the week; you'll use it whenever you've finished something, have an idea, or have experienced a mind-blowing discovery about God. OK, now get to planning! Remember to shout "Stellar!" when you're ready.

In order, have each Shuttle Team perform its quick-action skit before briefly explaining its part of the story. After every team presents, read the story summary together (found on page 3 of the *Mission Logs*) so everyone has a grasp of the Bible story's big picture.

Gather as a large group for a Mission Briefing, and discuss these questions:

★ How easy or difficult was it to express your verses in three seconds? Explain.

★ What stood out to you most from these Bible passages?

★ Which words would you use to describe God's creation? How far does it go?

★ During each voyage we take this week, we'll have a "Live It!," a truth about God that we can take and live out in our lives every day. Our "Live It!" today is "God's wondrous creativity has no limits! I can experience him everywhere." What does that mean to you?

Have a volunteer read aloud the Key Verse, Psalm 90:2, while the others follow along in the Bible or on page 3 of their *Mission Logs*: "Before the mountains were born or you brought forth the earth and the world, from everlasting to everlasting you are God."

Spend time throughout the day committing this verse to memory. Tomorrow you'll have a chance to recite it during *Outer Limits*. Remember, though, to do more than just memorize. Take time to think about what each word means.

Our wonder for the day: God's creativity is limitless. It's ever-moving in all directions, and was present even before he created the world and humans. Like our little moving snapshots, we are limited beings. But we can experience him everywhere because of who he is and how much he loves us. Now that's truly stellar!

As you dig into today's Bible story and Key Verse, leave the discussion open to questions that go a little deeper—such as what it means to be a Christian, who Jesus was, how someone gets into heaven, and so on. Use some students' curiosity, and others' prior knowledge, to foster discussion about the gospel.

Gauge where your students are, and make a decision about how far to proceed in the conversation. If you sense that a student is interested in committing to a relationship with Jesus, don't hesitate to step aside to pray with him or her as a volunteer continues leading the activity. Or, you may sense that it's best to offer an opportunity to the entire group to pray, asking Christ to forgive their sins and come into their hearts. Ask God to lead you in the right way through each of these valuable discussions. For ideas on helping invite students to Christ, see pages 26-28 of this Leader's Guide.

Additionally, encourage students to discover more about the gospel by checking out the "Expedition: Supernova" section on page 4 of their *Mission Logs*.

CONTEMPLATING THE JOURNEY

To give students a quiet opportunity to connect with God, guide them through this idea for contemplating today's Key Verse, Psalm 90:2.

Have students find a spot away from others. If possible, dim the lights. Quickly teach students sign language for the following words: *before, world, everlasting, God*.

Remind students to refer to page 4 of their *Mission Logs* for the Key Verse and sketches of each sign.

After students have learned the four signs, encourage them to spend the next few minutes in silence, connecting with God over the meaning of the psalm in their lives. As they contemplate the verse, they can continue using the sign language as part of their own prayer to God.

BEFORE
Put both hands out, with fingers touching. Your left hand should be at a slight slant, with the palm facing away from your body. The palm of your right hand should face your body. Pull your right hand back, leaving your left hand in place.

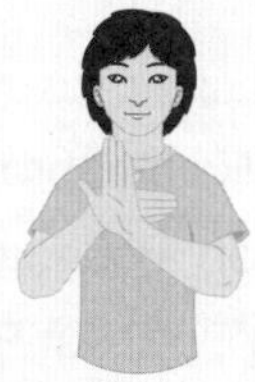

WORLD
Form a "W" with the middle three fingers of each hand. Make several horizontal circles. 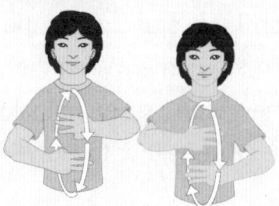

EVERLASTING
Bring right hand to forehead, with pointer finger, thumb, and pinky finger extended. Put out your middle two fingers briefly when hand is at your face (thumb near mouth), then tuck in first three fingers, leaving only thumb and pinky finger extended. Arc hand downward pushing down to waist and out, with your palm away from your body.

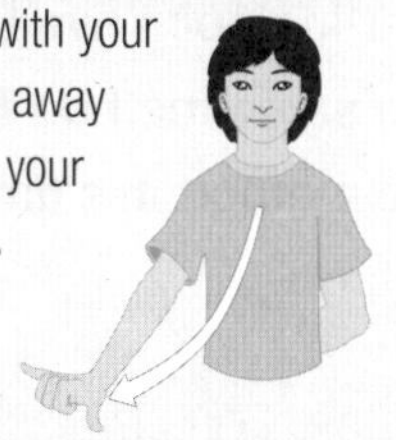

GOD
Put right arm out in front so it lines up with your body, right palm facing left and a little higher than your head. Look up, then bring your entire arm down so your hand passes and stops at your shoulders.

Expedition (45 minutes)

JOURNEY TO THE *OUTER LIMITS* – 15 minutes

It's time for our countdown to today's destination: Five, four, three, two, one…

Space Voyagers should now go to the Expedition portion of their Mission Logs on page 4.

Our destination today is the Rings of Saturn.

The rings that circle the planet Saturn are a creative mystery, even to astronomers. Saturn's rings make it unique among the other planets in our Solar System. There are three main rings, but more have been noticed lately. And, they're way different than any other type of ring—as big as the planet in diameter, with particles of water and ice ranging in size from microns (very small) to meters (very big).[1] To get to know our destination a little better, let's play a game we like to call "Sliding around the Rings of Saturn."

GAME: SLIDING AROUND THE RINGS OF SATURN – 20 minutes

Beforehand, mark off a large circular track with masking tape or cones. Select one point to be the starting line and mark it with different colored tape. The track lane should be wide enough for four or five students to be side-by-side. Have students get back in their Shuttle Teams and share the rules of the game: each Team must finish five laps around the track, with each member taking at least one lap. No one can go twice in a row. After each lap around the track, that member must "tag off" to the next member of his Team, who takes his place in the track (like in a relay race).

However, every lap must be completed using a different method. They won't know how they're moving around the track until you call it out, right before the first Team begins its second lap.

Have the first member of each Team stand within the track at the starting line, then call out **Walk backward**! to begin the game. When the walkers approach the starting line, call out **Hop on one leg!** The second racers should hop around the track. When they reach the starting line, call out **Knees!** For the fourth lap, call out **Roll!,** and for the fifth lap, **Hop backward!**

After all Teams have finished the five laps, congratulate everyone—but let them know the game's not quite over.

You're going to do that one more time. But this time, as long as you pass the starting point five times, you can do it however you'd like. Meaning, you can use the same method for every lap, and even the same person. And I don't choose the method this time. You do! Spend a moment strategizing now. [Pause.] Ready, set, go!

QUICK TIP!
A large area, such as a gymnasium, multi-purpose room, or outside lawn is needed in order to accommodate a track that can hold four or five students side by side. If you don't have a space large enough for the "Sliding around the Rings of Saturn" game, facilitate multiple rounds with just two or three teams going at a time. Then have the winning teams compete against each other in tournament fashion.

When all Teams have finished, discuss:

★ I didn't give any guidelines the second time around Saturn. In what ways were these two race experiences different?

★ What difference did it make that you could use creativity?

★ How could you have used even more creativity?

★ How can you compare this to God's creativity?

★ Where can we experience God's creativity? Be specific.

There's obviously a difference between limits and limitless creativity. Remember, you could do whatever you liked in the second version—including walking forward, or even cutting straight across the circle instead of going around. This reminds us of God, who created these mysterious, amazing rings of Saturn. Like Saturn's real rings, God's creativity is endless, with no real starting and ending points. We learned in our Bible story how deliberate and specific God was with his creation. We see that around the galaxy, and also in our personal lives. In fact, we can experience God everywhere.

SNACK – 15 minutes

Today's snack options are Meteor Munch, a delicious spacey concoction of popcorn, chocolate, and marshmallows, and Pizza Planets, an intergalactic treat that every student is sure to love. If running *Outer Limits* simultaneously with the elementary *Cosmic City*™ program, you may choose to gather all the children together for a large-group snack time. Otherwise, reference *The Shooting Star Drive-in Snack Guide* for specific instructions and recipes.

QUICK TIP!

If you choose to join the children participating in *Cosmic City*™ VBS, the snack is a great time to combine the groups. So that everyone has fun and gets to know students of other ages, create teams of five that include people from both programs. Teams should go through the entire snack time together every day.

To ensure that the snack time goes as smoothly as possible, ask for extra volunteers or parents to help during this part of the day. With more students in one area, there will naturally be more activity and noise. Volunteers should pay special attention to how students are interacting, handling the food and utensils, and following directions.

COSMIC CITY™ VBS Outer Limits Upper Elementary Guide

Experience (1 hour)

CRAFT: CREATION BRACELETS — 20 minutes

SUPPLIES
- [ ] Sample of completed craft
- [ ] 7' of suede cord per student
- [ ] 7 plastic bead (6x9 mm) per child (one of each color: yellow, blue, green, orange, red, brown, and white)
- [ ] Sewing scissors (at least one for every three students)
- [ ] Tape
- [ ] Tape measures or measuring tapes (at least one for every three students)

QUICK TIP!
If you are unable to find brown beads to represent Day 6, use black instead.

Voyage 1 Craft: Creation Bracelets

DO AHEAD
Cut seven feet of suede cord for each student. Create a sample *Creation Bracelet*. On a sheet of paper, write out the following key: "The Days of Creation: Day 1—yellow = light; Day 2—blue = sky; Day 3—green = land, sea, and plants; Day 4—orange = sun, moon, and stars; Day 5—red = birds and fish; Day 6—brown = animals, man, and woman; Day 7—white = rest, day of holiness."

We've been talking today about God's limitless creativity. We read in the Bible that he created the *entire* world in just seven days, one measly little week. Well, you're going to get a chance to make a bracelet that you can wear around your wrist or your ankle, or even attach to your backpack or keychain, that will remind you of what God did that very first week.

Each of your bracelets will have seven different colored beads, each representing a day of creation. Do you remember what God created on each day? Go through creation days one through seven, giving students a chance to remember or even look up in the Bible what happened on each day. Feel free to give them hints until they remember correctly.

Each day of creation will correspond with a bead in your bracelet. Here's what each color means. Refer to the key, then place it in a place where students can easily refer to it.

INSTRUCTIONS
1. Take a suede cord; each is about seven feet long.
2. Cut your strip into three 2-foot pieces and two 6-inch pieces.
3. Use one 6-inch piece to tie together the three 2-foot pieces. Make the knot about 4 inches from the end. Pull to make the knot tight.
4. Using tape, secure the end of your bracelet to the table, making it easier to braid.

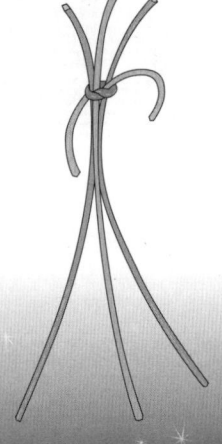

COSMIC CITY™ VBS Outer Limits Upper Elementary Guide

5. Braid together the three 2-foot pieces for about 1/2 inch. Then place your yellow bead onto the middle lace and continue braiding for another 1/2 inch.
6. Place your orange bead on the middle lace and continue braiding for another 1/2 inch. Continue this process until all seven creation beads have been braided, in order, onto your bracelet.
7. Once all seven beads are on your bracelet, continue braiding until your bracelet has reached your desired length. (Long enough to fit on your wrist or ankle.)
8. Finish by tying the remaining 6-inch piece in a tight knot at the end of your braid. Remove the tape from the bracelet.
9. Trim the unneeded ends. Be sure that there is enough suede remaining on each end to tie it comfortably.
10. Put the bracelet on, and have a friend securely tie the two ends together.

As you tie each other's bracelets, practice explaining what each bead represents. Then when you get home, explain each bead's significance to a different friend or family member. After a minute, give students the chance to show off their bracelets.

You have on your wrists a tangible reminder of God's creativity—it's unique, beautiful, and circular, just like Saturn's rings. Every time you look down and see the colors of creation, thank God for his limitless creativity and remember that you can experience him everywhere, because he's with you. There's no limit to what he can do in your life. Let's explore that more now.

LIVE IT! ACTIVITY – 25 minutes

Beforehand, set up five small stations around the room: Art, Storytelling, Music, Movement, and Logic. Clearly label each with an index card. Each station will offer students a creative way to worship God. At the Art station, set out markers, paper, clay or play dough, and other craft supplies. At the Storytelling station, set out paper, pens, crayons, markers, etc. At the Music station, set out sheet music of praise music, blank sheet music, pencils, and any musical instruments you have available (harmonica, recorder, acoustic guitar, and so on). No supplies are necessary for the Movement station. At the Logic station, set out index cards, pens, and about twenty toothpicks.

Ask students to open their *Mission Logs* to Voyage 1 on page 5. Here they'll find a description of each station and a row of boxes: places students can experience God (home, school, church, with friends, alone).

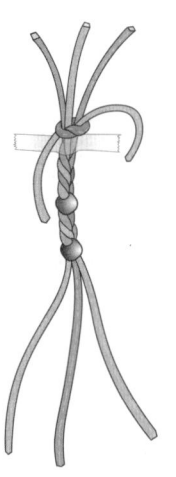

QUICK TIP!
Some of your students, especially some boys, may not be proficient at braiding. Ask your Guides and Tour Hosts to circulate among the class, taking time to help the students who may need a little extra hand. Also encourage your students to ask a Tour Host for help anytime they feel stuck or frustrated.

QUICK TIP!
Play some fun, energetic background music as the students work on their craft project. Praise and worship music or contemporary Christian music will set the right atmosphere.

Choose one of the boxes at the top of the page and answer this: What's one way you can worship God in this area of your life?

Discuss each of these areas with the students, coming up with different ways they can worship God in these areas of life. Prepare them for the following experience by encouraging them to be creative with their ideas. For instance, when they're alone, students might write a song about an aspect of God's creation. At school, they might experience God by relying on him to help them during a difficult test. At home, they might paint a picture of God's power in their lives and display it on the refrigerator.

Visit any or all of the stations. Choose the station that offers the skill that fits you best in worshipping God. Use the descriptions in your *Mission Logs* **to help you decide. Once you get to a station, randomly choose one of the boxes at the top of the page, and spend a few moments actively praising God for being with you in that area, so you can experience him. You may go to a new station and choose another box, or choose another box where you are. The point of these stations is to be creative, so do just that! Don't worry about what anyone else thinks; no one will be watching you. Focus only on growing closer to God, and praising him for the limitless love and creativity he displays in your life.**

Give students ten to fifteen minutes for this creative worship. Encourage them during this time to finish the prayer at the bottom of page 5 in their *Mission Logs*, and tell them when they have a minute left.

Have students find someone they haven't talked to yet, and discuss these questions, which are found on page 5 in their *Mission Logs*.

★ What was it like to worship God in this way?
★ What is one area in your life you want to know Jesus better?
★ How will you put today's "Live It!" into practice from now on?

In unison, have students shout out the **Live It!** together: **God's wondrous creativity has no limits! I can experience him everywhere!**

As we learned in our Bible story, God's wondrous creativity is limitless and huge. And, as we just experienced, we can grow close to him everywhere, in many different ways. Tonight, make sure to do one thing to respond to God's creativity and love for you.

Brainstorm a few ideas together, and then have students choose their favorite idea to write on the blank lines at the bottom of the "Back to Earth" take-home page of their *Mission Logs* (page 6), along with the other challenges.

Launch Farther!

We've deliberately designed these stations to be easy and require minimal preparation. However, if you have the time and resources, you might make the experience even more memorable by providing more complex supplies. For instance, include paints in the Art station, and set drop cloths underneath. For the Music station, plug in a CD player with instrumental music and attach headphones to the player. For the Movement station, set out streamers and several small foam balls. You might come up with other creative ideas to enhance the stations.

CLOSING ASSEMBLY – 15 minutes

Gather Space Voyagers back together in the general meeting area.

I know you've been wondering what's happening to the heroes from our drama this morning. Let's go warp speed right back into the action…

Actors perform the skit for Voyage 1: Part 2. The script for today's skit can be found on pages 92–93 of this Leader's Guide.

Tour Host gives announcements and includes any specific additional information.

Don't forget, Outer Limits begins at [time of meeting]. We'll see you then. Remember to bring in your money for the mission project. Also, take home today's "Back to Earth" page, and join in the activities with your family. You'll also choose which Cosmic Challenges you'll embark on before we meet again.

Thanks so much for being a great member of our space journey today. We've got many more exciting destinations to go. See you tomorrow for the next part of our adventure!

At the end of each day, students will take home only the day's "Back to Earth" Student Book page. They'll take what's left of the entire book home after Voyage 5. Have students write their names in marker on the cover of their *Mission Logs*, and count the books each afternoon to make sure you have the right number. You may also want several staplers available to students to staple that day's pages together at the end of each day. Store the books in a safe place every night. Choose a place where they're easily retrievable for the following day's **"Live It!"** activity, such as near the entrance to the large group area, a drawer with Bibles, or even the backseat of your car. As you begin each activity that requires the students use their Mission Logs, have the same volunteer leader be responsible for distributing the books to the right students and then recollecting them again.

You'll also want to order several extra student books ahead of time, as new students will likely join you as the week progresses. Check out www.cookvbs.com for ordering information.

QUICK TIP!

During the closing assembly announcement time, you may want to discuss more program logistics, such as carpools that have been set up. Encourage students to invite their friends to *Outer Limits*, and to let their parents know about the closing assembly on the final day, where everyone will celebrate together. You can customize the parent invitations found on the *Cosmic City*™ VBS CD-ROM.

Notes

Voyage 2: Desert Wonder

BIBLE STORY
God Provided Manna, Quail, and Water for the Israelites (Exod. 16:1–17, 31–36; 17:1–6)

KEY VERSE
The Lord will guide you always; he will satisfy your needs. (Isa. 58:11)

LIVE IT!
God's wondrous trustworthiness has no limits! I can be secure.

Exploration (1 hour, 15 minutes)

OPENING ASSEMBLY – 30 minutes

Outer Limits Leader welcomes students.

Welcome back, Voyagers! Yesterday you journeyed to the rings of Saturn—who knows where you'll end up today? One thing is for sure: you'll discover something amazing about God. First, settle in and enjoy more from The Outer Limits Theater Group.

Actors perform the skit for Voyage 2: Part 1. The script for today's skit can be found on pages 94–96 of this guide.

Cosmic City™ Tour Director or another adult gives an update on the daily mission project.

Share the Wonder: There Bibles for Brazil

Yesterday, we talked about a special project we're doing this week. We're sending children in Pernambuco, Brazil, books that have the part of the Bible that tells about Jesus. *Hold up the sample book.* Did any of you bring money to help? If so, let's collect it now. The books we're sending mean so much. Let me tell you about two little boys who received these books—their names are Italo and Gilvan, and they are seven years old. One day, missionaries were in their town giving

COSMIC CITY™ VBS Outer Limits Upper Elementary Guide

QUICK TIP!

Write the following questions on a whiteboard or large poster for students to use as a prompt in discussion with their partner. Then use this same poster every day to prompt students as they review the previous day's lesson with their partner (just be sure to update the Key Verse every day).

- Which challenge or challenges from yesterday's "Back to Earth" page did you do?
- What did you learn about yourself from completing it? About others? About God?
- With your partner, say yesterday's Key Verse (Ps. 90:2). If you need a little help reviewing, look it up in the Bible as you read it together.

Launch Farther!

If you've opted to facilitate an ongoing competition amongst Shuttle Teams, award each team a point for each member who can successfully recite the previous day's verse. Ask your Guides and adult Tour Hosts to go pair to pair to listen to each student recite it.

If you haven't set up a week-long competition but would still like to reward students for memorizing Key Verses, consider giving a small reward each day to students who can recite the previous day's Key Verse. Stickers, candy, or small token gifts/toys work well. (You can order *Cosmic City*™ themed stickers at www.cookvbs.com.)

---

away Bibles and the same books we're sending to Brazil. Italo and Gilvan were playing with a slingshot outside, so the missionary stopped to read some of the stories to them and their friends. They handed the two boys copies of the very book we're sending. The boys were so excited about all the stories they heard about Jesus! Soon, both boys said they wanted to be pastors when they grew up. The books they were given will help them learn about Jesus, which will help them prepare to be pastors one day. Keep bringing in your change to send more books to children like Italo and Gilvan.

Tour Host gives announcements and includes any specific additional information.

Remember, if you need anything at all today, please let one of the leaders know; we're here for you.

Have students meet in Voyager Pairs for challenge check-in. Give students one or two minutes to tell their partners which challenges from their "Back to Earth" page they accomplished, and what they learned from it—about themselves, others, or God. When finished sharing, have each pair say yesterday's Key Verse (Ps. 90:2) to each other. If they struggle saying it from memory, ask them to look it up in the Bible and review it together.

Tour Director, Tour Host, or teen Guide prays:

Lord, we learned a lot yesterday about your limitless creativity. Thank you that we can experience you everywhere; please help us grow closer to you in every area of our lives. Guide our adventures today as we visit another extreme destination and discover something new about you. In Jesus' name, amen.

Worship Blastoff

A leader plays the *Cosmic City*™ theme song. You can choose to play the DVD with guided motions, have students create their own movements to accompany the song, or do the following: **Get on your feet—it's time to sing our theme song. As you sing the verses, clap your hands. When the chorus comes, spin in a circle…and keep spinning!**

Rally *(optional)* – 15 minutes

If you choose this option, you can play the *Cosmic City*™ VBS *Praise Songs* CD or *Music and Promo* DVD for portions of this time and have a live worship band lead other parts. You may want to have the songs displayed on a screen using PowerPoint slides or an overhead.

Right now we're going to spend a few minutes worshipping God through

music. During this time, focus on nothing but the truth of the words you're singing. Celebrate how amazing God is!

Song suggestions:
★ *God Will Meet My Needs* (John DiModica, *Cosmic City*™ VBS *Praise Songs* CD or *Music and Promo* DVD)
★ *Before the Rocks Cry Out* (John DiModica, *Cosmic City*™ VBS *Praise Songs* CD or *Music and Promo* DVD)
★ *In Christ Alone* (Keith Getty and Stuart Townend)
★ *Shout to the Lord* (Darlene Zschech)
★ *Every Move I Make* (David Ruis)

You may read the following passages aloud in between songs, have a volunteer read the verses aloud, or say the Scripture together: Psalm 46:1 and Isaiah 41:10.

BIBLE STORY/KEY VERSE/LIVE IT! – 30 minutes

Have students form three Shuttle Teams and assign one of the sections of Scripture to each team: Team 1—Exodus 16:1–17; Team 2—Exodus 16:31–36; and Team 3—Exodus 17:1–6. Give each team paper and pens, and tell them their mission is to write a summary of their passage from the perspective of one of the following characters: Team 1: quail; Team 2: manna; and Team 3: water. What they write must capture the main points and action, but it has to be told from their character's viewpoint—including what their character might be thinking, observing, and feeling.

Give students five to ten minutes to write. Then, ask each team, beginning with Team 1, to read their story aloud.

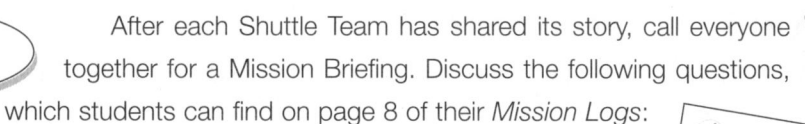

After each Shuttle Team has shared its story, call everyone together for a Mission Briefing. Discuss the following questions, which students can find on page 8 of their *Mission Logs*:

★ What was it like to tell the story from another point of view?
★ How does this change *your* view of the story? Of God? What did you notice that you might have missed?
★ What do we learn about God's trustworthiness in this Bible story?

Turn back to page 7 in your *Mission Log* and let's read the Bible story summary together. Choose three volunteers to read. After the story, read the Key Verse together: **"The Lord will guide you always; he will satisfy your needs (Isa. 58:11)."**

★ Why is it important to let God guide us and satisfy our needs?

QUICK TIP!
You may want to ask a Voyager to pray to begin your day together. If so, either give him or her a couple of suggestions—or allow the prayer to come spontaneously. Your students' prayers could surprise you (in a good way). But even if they don't, remember that God isn't impressed by our prayers, anyway; all he desires is a sincere heart.

QUICK TIP!
If you have a large number of students, give the same passage to more than one team. If you have a small number of students, assign one or two passages to a Shuttle Team.

Launch Farther!
If you're using the competition option, there will undoubtedly be more than three teams. In that case, it's okay to assign each passage to more than one team.

Launch Farther!
Have students go to their *Mission Logs*, where the Bible story is told in script form. Students can form groups of three and read through this script together, then discuss the questions, which are listed after the story.

- What makes you feel secure—like you can be confident that God wants the best for you—no matter what happens?
- What makes you feel insecure—like God isn't really in control of what's happening?
- What's the difference between being secure, and believing that nothing bad will ever happen to you? Give an example.
- Today's Live It! is: God's wondrous trustworthiness has no limits. How can this make you secure?

There's no limit to how much we can trust God. We never have to worry that he'll guide us in the wrong direction, or that we won't be taken care of. As the Israelites learned, God provides for our every need, and he guides us where we should go.

As you dig into today's Bible story and Key Verse, leave the discussion open to questions that go a little deeper—such as what it means to be a Christian, who Jesus was, how someone gets into heaven, and so on. Use some students' curiosity, and others' prior knowledge, to foster discussion about the gospel.

Gauge where your students are, and make a decision about how far to proceed in the conversation. If you sense that a student is interested in committing to a relationship with Jesus, don't hesitate to step aside to pray with him or her as a volunteer continues leading the activity. Or, you may sense that it's best to offer an opportunity to the entire group to pray, asking Christ to forgive their sins and come into their hearts. Ask God to lead you in the right way through each of these valuable discussions. For ideas on helping invite students to Christ, see pages 26–28 of this guide.

Additionally, encourage students to discover more about the gospel by checking out the "Expedition: Supernova" section on page 8 of their *Mission Logs*.

CONTEMPLATING THE JOURNEY (optional)

To give students a quiet opportunity to connect with God, guide them through this contemplative prayer idea.

Have students find a spot away from others. If possible, dim the lights. Give each student a small cup of water (paper or plastic). Tell them to reflect on the Scripture they've just explored, especially Isaiah 58:11. As they pray about the ways God meets their needs, they should slowly drink the glass of water as a symbol of their trust in God.

Remind students to refer to page 7 in their *Mission Logs* for the Key Verse. Also make sure each student has a Bible available.

Expedition (45 minutes)

JOURNEY TO THE *OUTER LIMITS* – 10 minutes

We've almost arrived at our next destination, and it's time for our countdown to reveal what it is: Five, four, three, two, one…

Voyagers should now go to the Expedition portion of their *Mission Logs* on page 8.

Our destination today is Mars. Direct students to look at the information and images about Mars on the Expedition page.

This is a really interesting place to be, since Mars is one of the most fascinating planets in the galaxy. You might know that Mars appears red; that's because of the amount of rust it has. Mars also has very extreme weather. The temperature is usually very cold, but it can vary from 207 degrees below zero to 80 degrees (only at the equator on a "summer" day). There are lots of violent storms, including hurricanes as large as the state of Texas. Lots of snow and ice cover the mountainous, cratered ground—but there's no water. And, finally, the air is only 1% as dense as our air on Earth.[2] So, in addition to the crazy weather, bitter cold, rugged terrain,[3] and lack of water…it's very hard to breathe where we're going.

To become more familiar with our destination, let's play a game called "Surviving the Surface of Mars."

GAME: SURVIVING THE SURFACE OF MARS – 20 minutes

Beforehand, put together a Mars survival kit. On a tray, set out any or all of the following items: small umbrella; stocking hat; an index card with the symbol for oxygen (O_2); sunglasses; winter gloves or mittens; stocking hats; wool socks; rope; boots; energy or granola bar; paper towels; sealed bag of water; small, round hard candy; adhesive bandage; rubber band; small candle; doctor's mask; pack of gum; pocket Bible; pen; and compass. (Feel free to add other items to the kit. Or if you have a hard time finding any of the above items, replace them with other items that may be useful for survival.) Cover the tray with a sheet and place it on a far side of the room. You may even want to place some sort of barrier (such as a table covered with a tablecloth) between the tray and the rest of the room so that students cannot simply look across the room and see the tray.

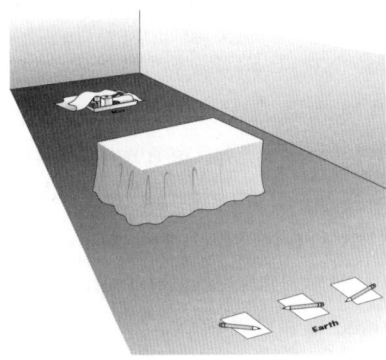

Ask Space Voyagers to gather around the tray, still covered by a sheet. **You're now on the surface of Mars. On this covered tray are all the things needed to survive here.**

Have students walk to the other side of the room. Set out one piece of paper and a pencil for each Shuttle Team of three to five students. **You're now on Earth, where you're safe. Form Shuttle Teams of three to five and sit down as soon as your team is formed.** Allow students about a minute to get into teams.

One by one, you're going to have to run back and forth from the Earth to Mars, writing one item on this paper each time. You can't write more than one

Launch Farther!

If you're conducting the optional week-long competition among Shuttle Teams, ask your students to join these same teams for this Mars survival game.

item on each trip, and you can't write any repeats. Only one person from each team can be running or writing at a time. The next team member can't take off for Mars until the previous member has finished writing the latest item on the list. You can cheer your teammates on but may not help them as they're writing. There should be no repeats on any team's list, and each team's goal is to include everything from the survival kit on their list. If your team thinks you've successfully listed every object, call out "Stellar!" to signal you've finished. Everyone must stop when they hear a team shout "Stellar." Then a leader will check your list against the actual survival kit. If the list isn't complete, then all teams can resume playing.

After the game is finished, discuss the following as a group:
* If you'd had only the items you listed, how well would you have survived on Mars? Explain.
* Why are *all* of these items needed to live on the surface of Mars?
* What do *you* need to live? How can you trust God to survive?

Wow, it's a good thing we don't actually live on Mars. We wouldn't feel safe at all. Sometimes that's how life on Earth can be too. Even if we're OK physically, we may feel like we're in an extreme storm with a friend—or out in the cold with our family. Or like we can't breathe at school. Life can be dangerous and unpredictable. We never know what'll happen, but we can be secure in God because he's wondrously trustworthy. We can know that he's in control, even when we don't understand why things happen the way they do.

SNACK – 15 minutes

Voyage 2 snack options are Planet Pops and Modern Manna. Planet Pops are a tasty and festive symbol of God's outer space wonder, and Modern Manna a reminder of God's provision for the Israelites in the desert. If running *Outer Limits* simultaneously with the elementary *Cosmic City*™ program, you may choose to gather all the children together for a large-group snack time. Otherwise, reference *The Shooting Star Drive-in Snack Guide* for specific instructions and recipes.

Experience (1 hour)

CRAFT: DUCT TAPE SURVIVAL KITS - 20 minutes

SUPPLIES
- ☐ Sample of completed craft
- ☐ 12.5' of duct tape per student
- ☐ Sewing scissors (at least one pair for every three students)
- ☐ Colored plastic tape
- ☐ Rulers (one per student)

Voyage 2 Craft: Duct Tape Survival Kits

DO AHEAD

Cut 17 8-inch long pieces and two 7-inch long pieces of duct tape for each student. Hang each piece at the end of a table or chair to make it easy for students to quickly peel off and use. Create a sample *Duct Tape Survival Kit*.

Just as it would take a survival kit filled with specialized supplies to survive on Mars, we also need certain items to survive here on Earth. Food, water, shelter . . , and we could probably add a few things to the list that would help us survive physically. But what does it take to survive *spiritually*? We're going to really explore that question in a few minutes, but first we're going to create a *Duct Tape Survival Kit*, a safe place to hold the things we value most.

INSTRUCTIONS

1. Lay an 8-inch piece of duct tape sticky side up on the table.
2. Lay another 8-inch piece of duct tape sticky side up next to the first piece, overlapping about 1/4 inch.
3. Add two more pieces of duct tape, creating four rows.
4. Now place an 8-inch piece of duct tape right on top of the first row of tape, sticky sides together.

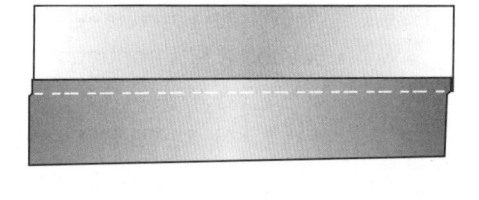

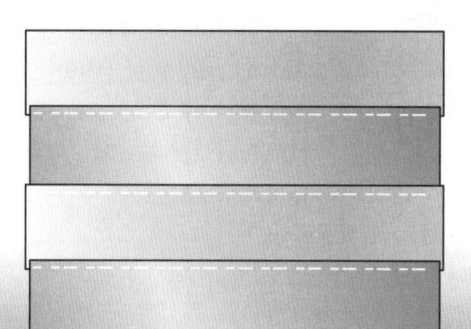

QUICK TIP!

The most time-intensive part of today's craft will be pre-cutting the duct tape. Plan on coming early to do the cutting. The process will go much more quickly if you're able to recruit several teen or adult volunteers to join you. If space allows, bring in one or two long tables, place them along the edges of the room, and hang the pre-cut tape pieces along the tables' edges.

QUICK TIP!

As you go through the first few instructions, model each step and have students follow along with you.

COSMIC CITY™ VBS Outer Limits Upper Elementary Guide

QUICK TIP!

Play some fun, energetic background music as the students work on their craft project. The *Cosmic City™ Praise Songs* CD is a great option. You can order CDs at www.cookvbs.com.

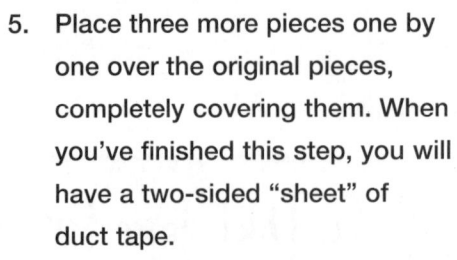

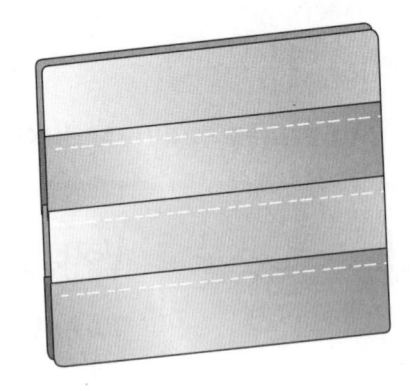

5. Place three more pieces one by one over the original pieces, completely covering them. When you've finished this step, you will have a two-sided "sheet" of duct tape.
6. Make another "sheet" like the first by repeating steps one through five.
7. Line up your two "sheets," and trim all around to make a neat rectangle.
8. Cut two 7-inch long pieces of duct tape and one 8-inch piece.
9. Join the two "sheets" together by placing each 7-inch piece along the two shorter edges of the rectangle and folding them, sticky side in, along the edge to create a finished crease. Do the same with the 8-inch piece along the bottom of the rectangle.
10. To create handles for your survival kit, cut two pieces of duct tape, each 12 inches long. Fold each piece in half lengthwise so the sticky side is inside.
11. Now tape the ends of the handles securely to the inside of the bag.
12. Using colored plastic tape, create your initials (first and last name), and stick them to the front side of your survival kit. This will set your kit apart from the others.

You've just created something that'll make every day a little easier; it'll hold all sorts of important things for you. It should also remind you of God, because just as it holds your things securely, God holds you securely. He'll always guide you and satisfy all your needs. Let's continue to discuss that.

LIVE IT! ACTIVITY – 25 minutes

Have students continue to hold their duct tape survival kits.

You made these kits to hold the things you value. And what's more valuable than those things that help you to survive spiritually? So now you're going to also make this your spiritual survival kit—SSK. Basically, what do you need to keep you following Jesus?

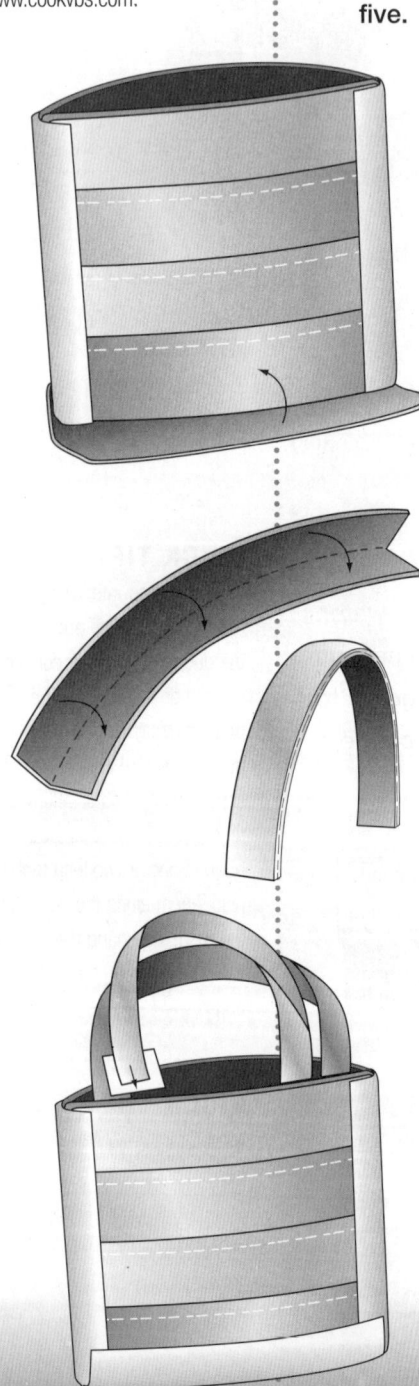

First of all, write our Key Verse, Isaiah 58:11, on a slip of paper and put it in your SSK. See, already you have something that reminds you to trust God. What else would remind you to trust God to keep you safe, stick by you, take away your sin, comfort you, save you, smooth you out, energize you, and more?

Set out a large collection of everyday items (some may be from the Mars survival kit you used in the game). Also include tape, cotton balls, paper clips, glitter, star stickers, pieces of sandpaper, pebbles, batteries, tissue, erasers, and toothpicks.

Have students read the list of items and purposes on page 9 in their *Mission Logs*. They can then choose whatever spiritual survival items they want, and put these things in their bags.

Now, get together in Shuttle Teams of three. I want each Voyager to share what items you picked and why.

Have Shuttle Teams discuss the following questions, which they can find in their *Mission Logs* on page 9:

★ What do you need to survive spiritually?
★ What's one area of your life where you need to feel secure?
★ How will you trust God to guide you and satisfy your needs?

God's wondrous trustworthiness has no limits; you can be 100% secure. God sent his Son Jesus to the dangerous planet of Earth so that we could not just survive, but thrive in a relationship with him. Just as God provided food and water for the Israelites, he'll provide for your needs—even if you feel like you're wandering around Mars without a survival kit. Trust him!

CLOSING ASSEMBLY – 15 minutes

Let's catch up with our friends, who were in a little bit of danger themselves last time we saw them…

Actors perform the skit for Voyage 2: Part 2. The script for today's skit can be found on pages 97–98 of this guide.

Tour Host gives announcements, including any specific information in addition to the following:

QUICK TIP!

Your preteens should be well able to grasp the abstract meaning of the symbolic items, especially with the help of the *Mission Logs*. However, if you'd like to be even clearer, make small paper labels and set them next to the items (such as: "God will comfort you" next to the adhesive bandage and "God will stick by you" next to the tape).

QUICK TIP!
If time allows, encourage students to spend a few minutes finishing the prayer at the bottom of page 9 in their *Mission Logs*.

As always, remember to bring your mission project money tomorrow. And be here at or before [time your group begins] so you're ready when we begin our third Voyage into the *Outer Limits*. Also, take home today's "Back to Earth" page 10 and experience the activities with your family. You'll also choose which Cosmic Challenges you'll embark on before we meet again.

Get some rest tonight, because we'll be in the middle of another breathtaking quest tomorrow—and you'll need all your energy. Stellar!

Notes

Notes

COSMIC CITY™ VBS Outer Limits Upper Elementary Guide

Voyage 3: Healing Wonder

BIBLE STORY
Jesus Heals a Paralyzed Man (Luke 5:17–26)

KEY VERSE
You are the God who performs miracles; you display your power among the peoples. (Ps. 77:14)

LIVE IT!
God's wondrous power has no limits! I can put my faith in him.

Exploration (1 hour, 15 minutes)

OPENING ASSEMBLY – 30 minutes

Tour Director welcomes students.

We had such a stellar Voyage yesterday, didn't we? How great it's been to see what you're all doing in your Shuttle Teams, Mission Briefings, and also those quiet times when you're alone with God. We're in for more excitement today, right after this look at what our favorite Teens and Robot are up to…

Actors perform the skit for Voyage 3: Part 1. The script for today's skit can be found on pages 99–101 of this Leader's Guide.

Tour Director or another adult gives an update on the daily mission project.

Share the Wonder: There—Bibles for Brazil

As you know, this week we're collecting money to send part of the Bible to children in Brazil. *Hold up the sample book.* **Did anyone bring money to help today? We'll collect it now.** While we do that, let me tell you what Pastor Francisco said about how much these books mean to the people where he lives. He said that the people are very poor, and there are no jobs available for them to make money.

COSMIC CITY™ VBS Outer Limits Upper Elementary Guide

QUICK TIP!
Write the following questions on a whiteboard or large poster for students to use as a prompt in discussion with their partner:

- Which challenge or challenges from yesterday's "Back to Earth" page did you do?
- What did you learn about yourself from completing it? About others? About God?
- With your partner, say yesterday's Key Verse (Isa. 58:11) to each other. If you need a little help reviewing, look it up in the Bible as you read it.

Launch Farther!

If you've opted to facilitate an ongoing competition amongst Shuttle Teams, award each team a point for each member who can successfully recite the previous day's verse. Ask your teen and adult volunteers to go pair to pair to listen to each student recite them.

If you haven't set up a week-long competition but would still like to reward students for memorizing Key Verses, consider giving a small reward each day to students who can recite the previous day's Key Verse. Stickers, candy, or small token gifts/toys work well. (You can order *Cosmic City*™ themed stickers at www.cookvbs.com.)

They can barely pay for food, so getting a Bible is almost impossible! When a new Christian comes to Pastor Francisco's church, he wants to give them a Bible, but has none to give. The people who come to him want Bibles and need them. Their friends and families don't like that they are following God, and treat them in terrible ways. So these people need to know more about God so they can stay strong when hard things happen and can explain what they believe. It's not just grown-ups that need Bibles for these reasons—even the children need them. As you can tell from what Pastor Francisco said, the books we are raising money for are very, very important. So bring your change tomorrow if you'd like to help.

Adult leader gives announcements, being sure to include any additional information related to your specific program.

As always, we want you to have fun and focus on God during today's Voyage. Tell one of the Tour Hosts or Guides if you need anything throughout the day.

Have students meet in Voyager Pairs for challenge check-in. Give students one or two minutes to tell their partners which challenges from their "Back to Earth" page they accomplished, and what they learned from it—about themselves, others, or God. When finished sharing, have each pair say yesterday's Key Verse (Isa. 58:11) to each other. If they struggle saying it from memory, ask them to look it up in the Bible and review it together.

Tour Director, Tour Host, or teen Guide prays:

Heavenly Father, you're our Ultimate Guide, and we're secure in trusting you. Thank you for holding us safe and satisfying our needs. Guide us today as we explore the galaxy in search of more truths about you. In Jesus' name, amen.

Worship Blastoff

A leader plays the *Cosmic City*™ theme song. You can choose to play the *Cosmic City*™ *Music and Promo* DVD with guided motions, have students create their own movements to accompany the song, or do the following: **Hope you're ready to sing our extra-stellar theme song. This time, snap your fingers during the verses and stomp your feet during the chorus.**

Rally *(optional)* – 15 minutes

If you choose this option, you may play the *Cosmic City*™ *Praise Songs* CD for portions of this time and have a live worship band lead other parts. As on previous days, you may choose to display each song's lyrics on a screen (or even a light-colored wall) using an overhead or projector and PowerPoint slides.

Let's praise God for being limitlessly creative and trustworthy. Ask God to give you a humble and thankful heart as we sing these songs of worship.

Song suggestions:
- ★ *My God Does Miracles* (Phil Reynolds, *Cosmic City*™ VBS *Praise Songs* CD and *Cosmic City*™ *Music and Promo* DVD)
- ★ *God of Power* (Phil Reynolds, *Cosmic City*™ VBS *Praise Songs* CD and *Cosmic City*™ *Music and Promo* DVD)
- ★ *Agnus Dei* (Michael W. Smith)
- ★ *God of Wonders* (Marc Byrd and Steve Hindalong)
- ★ *Here I Am to Worship* (Tim Hughes)

You may read aloud the following passages in between songs, have a volunteer read the verses aloud, or say the Scripture together: Exodus 15:11 and Isaiah 25:1.

BIBLE STORY/KEY VERSE/LIVE IT! – 30 minutes

Give everyone a Bible and have ten students read aloud Luke 5:17-26—*backward*, starting with verse 26, then verse 25, then verse 24, and so on. You'll want to specifically assign one verse to each of the ten and line them up in order at the front of the room before the reading begins.

OK, I think we *really* need a Mission Briefing after that.

Discuss the following:
- ★ What was it like to read the passage that way?
- ★ How do we sometimes experience life "backward"— the wrong way?
- ★ What do you do to make sure things go the right way?

Now, read Luke 5:17-26 again, this time from start to finish. You will want students to read the Bible Story Summary on page 11 in their *Mission Logs*. Then have a volunteer read aloud the Key Verse found at the top of the same *Mission Log* page while everyone follows along: **"You are the God who performs miracles; you display your power among the peoples (Ps. 77:14)."**

- ★ **Sum up the message of these passages in five words? Write this on page 12 in your *Mission Log*.**

God has the power to do anything—like completely heal someone, as he does in this story, create the entire world out of nothingness, or make the sky rain bread. God's miracles display his power, and lead us to put our faith in him. And

Launch Farther!

Try something unexpected during the Worship Rally: instead of singing one of the songs, speak the words together. This'll reveal new meaning to the students and help them worship God at a deeper level.

QUICK TIP!

These questions are also listed in the students' *Mission Logs* on page 12; you may have them discuss the questions with someone they haven't talked to yet, then gather again with the large group.

QUICK TIP!

As you talk about a relationship with Jesus, keep the following in mind (and on your heart):

- Focus on the true meaning of the gospel.
- Help Christian students articulate their faith, and give them an opportunity to renew their intimacy with Christ.
- Encourage other students to ask questions, and give them an opportunity to know Christ for perhaps the first time.
- Ask God to lead you in the most appropriate way through each of these valuable discussions. For ideas on helping invite students to Christ, see page 26 of this guide.
- Additionally, encourage students to discover more about the gospel by checking out the "Expedition: Supernova" section on page 12 of their *Mission Logs*.

when we do put our faith in him, we can know that he'll help us live the right way every day. The paralyzed man put his faith in Jesus, and Jesus healed him. We can follow this example.

✶ What does it mean to have faith in Jesus? How about being in a relationship with Jesus? How does someone come to have a relationship with Jesus?

✶ How would you describe your own relationship with Jesus? How do you want it to change, if at all?

God loves us so much that he wants to be with us forever, even after we die. So he sent his Son Jesus Christ to Earth to be fully human and fully God, at the same time. Jesus never sinned; he never did anything that made his Father sad. But even still, he died on the cross for all of our sins, for all the wrong things you and I have done. God resurrected Jesus from the dead, destroying sin's power over any of us. We can experience a close, intimate relationship with Jesus. All it takes is acknowledging what Jesus did for us and inviting him to live in us.

Say the following prayer, pausing for students to repeat after you, either silently or aloud:

Jesus, thank you so much for dying on the cross and rising again, so that my sins are forgiven and I can have eternal life with you in heaven. Please enter my life and, by your power, help me not to sin—but instead trust and obey you. Thank you for loving me so much that I can be in a relationship with you. In Jesus' name, amen.

CONTEMPLATING THE JOURNEY (optional)

To give students a quiet opportunity to connect with God, guide them through this idea for contemplating God's power in their lives, and how they might put their faith in him.

Have students find a spot away from others. If possible, dim the lights. Give each student a small lump of clay or modeling dough. Have them think and pray about God's power. As they do, they should mold the clay into something that represents their response to God's power. For instance, they might shape a smiley face, someone kneeling, or an open hand.

Remind students to refer to page 11 in their *Mission Logs* for the Key Verse. Also make sure each student has a Bible available.

Expedition (45 minutes)

JOURNEY TO THE *OUTER LIMITS* – 10 minutes

We're ready for the countdown to the reveal of our destination: Five, four, three, two, one...

Voyagers should now go to the Expedition portion of their *Mission Logs* on page 12.

Our destination today is the Sun. Direct students to look at the information and images of the Sun on the Expedition page.

This is pretty much the ultimate, extreme destination. Here are some "Suntastic" facts: The Sun holds several planets in orbit,[4] and is the major power behind all of Earth's weather[5]...even though they're 93 million miles away from each other. The Sun's total volume is *1,300,000* times Earth's, and its surface area is the same as *11,990* Earths.[6] Oh, and get this—the Sun's energy comes from its core, which can be as hot as 25 million degrees. When energy comes out of the Sun as solar wind, it travels at about a million miles per hour. [7]

That's some major power! Let's take a closer look in this game, "Seeing the Sun."

GAME: SEEING THE SUN — 20 minutes

Beforehand, write on slips of paper different superpowers. For instance, defying gravity, withstanding great heat, super-human strength, electricity-sparking hair, super-speed, etc. Give each student a slip of paper, making sure no one else sees it. Set up a "meteor field" made of chairs, scattered throughout your space.

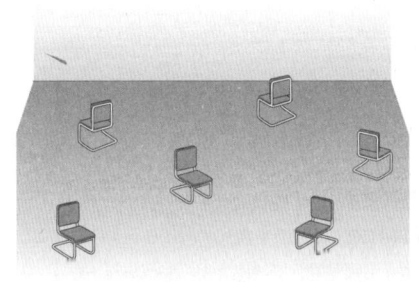

If we were near the Sun right now, we'd have to have some incredible powers. Let's try to figure out what each person's powers are. Students will take turns traveling from one end of the "meteor field" to the other, demonstrating their superpowers as they go. All other students will be seated in the chairs scattered throughout the "meteor field." If your group is smaller than 15, one student can travel at a time. If your group is larger, then several students (or even an entire Shuttle Team) can traverse the "meteor field" at once.

Here are the guidelines: You must not directly ask or tell about a superpower. The only way you can discover other Voyagers' powers is to pick up on hints they're giving. You're responsible, using only your actions, to give hints while you complete the mission: to travel through the meteor field—the scattered chairs and people spread across the room—while a *really* strong magnetic field tries to pull you backward. While on your mission, you cannot speak unless it's in direct response to a question asked by another student. You must use your superpower while you're traveling to the other side of the meteor field.

Have students take turns doing the mission (going through the meteor field, resisting the magnetic field). Whenever a student's power is discovered, have the guessing student shout "Stellar!"

QUICK TIP!
If you have a large group, form several Shuttle Teams, with every member of a team possessing the same power and acting and guessing simultaneously. If your group is small, no worries. This game works just as well with three students as it does with 50.

QUICK TIP!
Demonstrate the game as you explain the rules to your students. Choose a simple superpower like flying, and model how the game is played, allowing students to ask you questions just as they will when the activity officially begins.

After everyone has had a chance to journey through the "meteor field," end the game and discuss the following questions in a Mission Briefing:

- What was it like trying to discover these powers?
- In real life, why couldn't any of us get near enough to touch the Sun?
- What kind of limits do we have as humans?
- How does it make you feel to know that God's power has no limits?
- How does knowing God's power has no limits change the way you might live your life?

We've learned that the Sun has an unbelievable amount of power. But we know that God—who created the Sun—is even more powerful. His power has no limits, which he's shown through miracles. And when God works his power in our lives, something awesome happens: People don't really see us; they see God's power in us, through the ways we act and respond. On our own, we're not capable of doing anything miraculous or truly powerful. And just as you were trying to figure out what others could do in this game, we should always be looking for what God wants to do through those around you.

SNACK – 15 minutes

Today's snack options are Sun Bursts, which remind us of God's power as seen in creation, and Pudding Pop Walk, a chocolatey representation of today's Bible story. If running *Outer Limits* simultaneously with the elementary *Cosmic City*™ program, you may choose to gather all the children together for a large-group snack time. Otherwise, reference *The Shooting Star Drive-in Snack Guide* for specific instructions and recipes.

Launch Farther!

If you're implementing the competitive component throughout the week, you might have Shuttle Teams gather points for each correct guess made by a member of the team, then add those collective points to their overall score.

Experience (1 hour)

CRAFT: SONSHINE REFLECTORS – 20 minutes

SUPPLIES
- Sample of completed craft
- Round mirrors, 2" in diameter (one per student)
- Blue, black, yellow, orange, and red craft foam (2 mm thick)
- Scissors (one pair per student)
- Rubber cement (one bottle for every three to five students)
- Magnet tape
- Ruler (for prep only)
- Hardback books (one per student, to help craft remain flat while glue dries) (optional)

Voyage 3 Craft: Sonshine Reflectors

DO AHEAD
Cut 3 x 3-inch squares of blue and/or black craft foam (one square per student). Cut 1/2 x 5 1/2-inch strips of yellow, red, and/or orange craft foam (one strip per student). Cut 1-inch long strips of magnet tape (one strip per student). Place all of these supplies in neat piles on the craft table, making them easy for students to access.

Okay, Voyagers, let's go back to thinking about the Sun for a minute. Not only does it produce heat, but also light. And you know what? When we put our faith in God and allow his power to work in our lives, we reflect the brightest light of all—God's light. Let's all say it together…Stellar!

You're going to create a *Sonshine Reflector* that you can put up at home, or in a locker, keep in your bag, or even give to a friend.

INSTRUCTIONS
1. Choose one foam square, one foam strip, one mirror, and one magnet. Take these supplies back to your seat.
2. Cut small triangles from your bright-colored foam strip to use as sun rays. You may even want to cut three or four triangles from your strip and then trade strips with someone who has a different color. Then you will have more than one color of sun rays on your *Sonshine Reflector*. Remember, your sun ray triangles can be different sizes.
3. Peel the paper off your magnet and stick the magnet to the center of your foam square. Press the magnet against the foam for several seconds, allowing it to stick.
4. Now place your round mirror in the

QUICK TIP!
The most time-intensive part of today's craft will be pre-cutting the foam and magnets. As with yesterday's craft, plan on coming early to do the cutting, and recruit several teen or adult volunteers to join you to make the process go much more quickly.

QUICK TIP!
Carefully read all warnings and precautions on the rubber cement bottles before placing them out for students to use. Then read all pertinent warnings aloud to your students before they begin the craft. You may even choose to have adult volunteers apply the rubber cement to each craft.

COSMIC CITY™ VBS Outer Limits Upper Elementary Guide

QUICK TIP!
The rubber cement will take about 30 minutes to dry. Have students leave their finished craft at the craft table until the end of this day's program. Be sure they remember to pick up their crafts before leaving for the day.

Also, to keep the mirrors from sliding off-center while they dry, place a hardback book (nothing too valuable) on top of each craft while it dries.

QUICK TIP!
Play some fun, energetic background music as the students work on their craft project. The *Cosmic City™ Praise Songs* CD is a great option. You can order CDs at www.cookvbs.com.

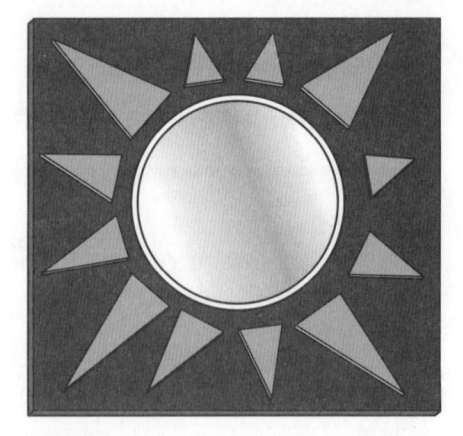

center of your foam square on the opposite side from the magnet.

5. Then arrange your triangular sun rays around the mirror so that it resembles the sun. Each person's sun will look different.
6. Once your mirror and sun rays are positioned as you'd like them, carefully begin gluing your mirror, using the rubber cement, onto the foam square. Hold the mirror firmly against the foam for about 10 seconds to let the glue begin drying.
7. Next, glue each sun ray in the desired position around your mirror.

> When you've finished your Sonshine Reflector, talk with your Voyage Partner about how you can reflect God's power and light in what you do every day:
> ★ How can you reflect God's light when your parent asks you to do something around the house?
> ★ How about when you're at school or playing with friends?

After a minute or two of discussion, give students the chance to show off their mirrors to the rest of the group.

Put this mirror up somewhere where you'll see it and remember that you want people to look at you, but see God's light instead. This'll also be a reminder to put your faith in God's wondrous power.

LIVE IT! ACTIVITY – 25 minutes

The Sun–what a miraculous thing! In a way, so is our faith, because it's not like we can even see God in the same way we see the Sun. However, we see his power all around us. Turn back to your Voyage Partner. I want you to take turns telling each other one way you'd like to have more faith in God. It might be for a family member who's sick, for better effort in school, or for a friendship that's not doing well. As you talk, hold your mirrors—not so your partner is reflected in it, but so he or she can be reminded of what it means to reflect God's light. When you've finished talking, shout that key word, "Stellar!"

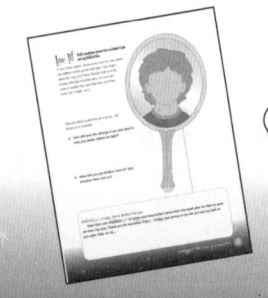

Have students read each question from page 13 in their *Mission Logs*; then discuss each one as a large group. Give students time to write their answers and ideas before the next question is read.

★ How will your life change if you ask God to help you better reflect his light?

COSMIC CITY™ VBS Outer Limits Upper Elementary Guide

★ How will you put today's "Live It!" into practice from now on? (Live It!: God's wondrous power has no limits! I can put my faith in him.)

Afterward, have one or more Voyager volunteers pray aloud that God would display his power in their lives as they daily put their faith in him. You may also encourage each student to finish the prayer on the bottom of *Mission Log* page 13.

CLOSING ASSEMBLY – 15 minutes

After our sunny adventure today, I'm sure you want to know what's going on with our three favorite characters…

Actors perform the skit for Voyage 3: Part 2. The script for today's skit can be found on page 102 of this guide.

Tour Host gives announcements and includes any additional information specific to your program:

Set out your money for the mission projects today when you go home so you remember to bring it with you tomorrow, when you arrive by [time your group will start]. Also, take home today's *"Back to Earth"* page and experience the activities with your family. You'll also choose which Cosmic Challenges you'll embark on before we meet again.

Thanks for a wonderful journey to the *Outer Limits*! We'll see you tomorrow for yet another cosmic expedition.

Notes

Voyage 4: Water Wonder

BIBLE STORY
Jesus Walks on Water (Matt. 14:22–33)

KEY VERSE
All things are possible with God. (Mark 10:27)

LIVE IT!
God's wondrous plan has no limits! I can live boldly.

Exploration (1 hour, 15 minutes)

OPENING ASSEMBLY – 30 minutes

Outer Limits Leader welcomes students.

Greetings, courageous Space Voyagers. Yesterday you traveled to the Sun and learned some pretty incredible things about God. There's another wonder waiting just beyond the closest star. First, though, here's the next chapter in our ongoing space saga …

Actors perform the skit for Voyage 4: Part 1. The script for today's skit can be found on pages 103–105 of this Leader's Guide.

Outer Limits Leader or another adult gives an update on the daily mission project.

Share the Wonder: There—Bibles for Brazil

Do any of you remember our special project this week? We're raising money to send a part of the Bible to children in Brazil. *Hold up the sample book.* If anyone brought some change today, we'll collect it now. While we do that, let me tell you that it isn't just the children who appreciate these books. Some adults do too! I'd like to share about a lady named Susy. She had been trying to read the Word of God, but it was always hard for her to understand what she was reading,

QUICK TIP!
Write the following questions on a whiteboard or large poster for students to use as a prompt in discussion with their partner. Then use this same poster every day to prompt students as they review the previous day's lesson with their partner (just be sure to update the Key Verse every day).
- Which challenge or challenges from yesterday's "Back to Earth" page did you do?
- What did you learn about yourself from completing it? About others? About God?
- With your partner, say yesterday's Key Verse (Ps. 77:14) to each other. If you need a little help reviewing, look it up in the Bible as you read it together.

QUICK TIP!
By this point in the week, you have a firm grasp of how things are running. Feel free to add any announcements that have become necessary or omit those that are no longer needed.

and most of the time she couldn't. A missionary told her about some of these books we are sending. She was given one, and now she not only has her own Bible, but she can also understand what she's reading and learn about the Lord! These books mean so much to the people of Brazil. There's still tomorrow for us to collect enough to send even more books. So let's see how many more we can send! Don't forget to bring any change you'd like to give.

Tour Host gives announcements. Be sure to include any additional information specific to your program.

As we go to the *Outer Limits* today, remember our travel guidelines: be respectful, focus on God, and have fun! If you have questions at any point, get a leader's attention; we'd love to help you.

Have students meet in Voyager Pairs for challenge check-in. Give students one or two minutes to tell their partners which challenges from their "Back to Earth" page they accomplished, and what they learned from it—about themselves, others, or God. When finished sharing, have each pair say yesterday's Key Verse (Ps. 77:14) to each other. If they struggle saying it from memory, ask them to look it up in the Bible and review it together.

Tour Director, Tour Host, or teen Guide prays:

Dear God, you're so powerful in the universe and in our daily lives. Don't let us miss any of your miracles so that we may praise you and put our faith in you. Work in our hearts and minds today as we come to understand you better. In Jesus' name, amen.

Worship Blastoff

A leader plays the *Cosmic City*™ theme song. You can choose to play the *Cosmic City*™ *Music and Promo* DVD with guided motions, have students create their own movements to accompany the song, or do the following: **Get on your feet—it's time to sing our theme song. As you sing the verses, clap your hands. When the chorus comes, spin in a circle … and keep spinning!**

Rally *(optional)* **– 15 minutes**

If you choose this option, you will play the *Cosmic City*™ VBS *Praise Songs* CD or *Cosmic City*™ VBS *Music and Promo* DVD for portions of this time and have a live worship band lead other parts.

God is so great! Let's respond to his greatness by singing songs of worship. Tune out everything and everyone around you, and concentrate on telling God how awesome he is.

Song suggestions:
- ✸ *All Things are Possible* (John DiModica, *Cosmic City*™ VBS CD and DVD)
- ✸ *You Are* (Darren Roose, *Cosmic City*™ VBS CD and DVD)
- ✸ *How Great Is Our God* (Chris Tomlin)
- ✸ *Open the Eyes of My Heart*, Lord (Paul Baloche)
- ✸ *Days of Elijah* (Robin Mark)

You may read the following passages aloud in between songs, have a volunteer read the verses aloud, or say the Scriptures together: Ephesians 3:12, 2 Timothy 1:7, and Matthew 19:26.

BIBLE STORY/KEY VERSE/LIVE IT! – 30 minutes

Form Shuttles Teams of three to five people. In your group, take turns telling a one-minute story about the most courageous thing you've ever done. Perhaps it was talking in front of a large group, hiking a mountain, or even apologizing to someone. I'm going to give you a few seconds to think of your story.

After about 30 seconds of "think time," begin timing students, letting them know when each minute is up so they can move on. After everyone has shared a story, have a volunteer read Matthew 14:22-23 aloud to the entire group.

Discuss the following questions together:
- ✸ What kind of story would Peter have told? How was his story different from or similar to ours?
- ✸ How would you have felt and what would you have done if you were Peter, and why?
- ✸ What does this story show us about what it means to be bold?
- ✸ How and why does God help us be bold?

Together as a large group, have students read aloud the Key Verse on page 15 of their *Mission Logs*: **"All things are possible with God" (Mark 10:27).** You also may choose three volunteers to read aloud the Bible story summary on page 15 of their *Mission Logs*.

Give each Shuttle Team a dictionary, paper, and pens, and have students look up the definitions of key words from the Key Verse. You may have students choose the key words, or ask them to use the following words, which are listed on page 16 in their *Mission Logs*: "all," "things," "possible," "with," and "God." Then give each Shuttle Team a couple of minutes to rephrase the verse in their own way, using different words. They can record their definitions in the *Mission Logs*.

Have each Shuttle Team share its rephrased Key Verse. Afterward, discuss:
- ✸ How easy or difficult was it to rephrase the Key Verse with new words?

QUICK TIP!
To spark students' ideas, tell a story of your own, or have an adult or teen volunteer share one of theirs.

Launch Farther!
Have Voyagers form pairs and read through the re-told Bible story on page 15 in their *Mission Logs*. Then have them read the account in Matthew 14:22–23. Finally, ask pairs to discuss the questions, which are also listed on that page.

QUICK TIP!
It might be difficult for students to find alternative words for "God" in the dictionary; however, encourage them to use other names for God such as Lord, Heavenly Father, and so on.

QUICK TIP!
If you have a large number of students, skip the dictionary activity; giving everyone time to tell their courage stories will take long enough. Have someone read aloud the Key Verse, then move right to the second discussion question.

★ When you hear the words "God's plan," what's your instant reaction?
★ What are characteristics of God's wondrous plan that allow us to live boldly? I'll start us off with a couple: God's wondrous plan is perfect, and God's wondrous plan is for our best....

Our wonder for the day: God's wondrous plan has no limits! I can live boldly. What an out-of-this-world concept! Just like this Key Verse can be stated in many different ways while keeping the same meaning, God can take us in many different directions while keeping the same overall plan. After all, God loves us more than anyone else does or ever will—and he knows what's best for us. Therefore, we can live courageously!

As you dig into today's Bible story and Key Verse, leave the discussion open to questions that go a little deeper—such as what it means to be a Christian, who Jesus was, how someone gets into heaven, and so on. Use some students' curiosity, and others' prior knowledge, to foster discussion about the gospel.

Gauge where your students are, and make a decision about how far to proceed in the conversation. If you sense that a student is interested in committing to a relationship with Jesus, don't hesitate to step aside to pray with him or her as a volunteer continues leading the activity. Or, you may sense that it's best to offer an opportunity to the entire group to pray, asking Christ to forgive their sins and come into their hearts. Ask God to lead you in the right way through each of these valuable discussions. For ideas on helping invite students to Christ, see pages 26–28 of this Leader's Guide.

Additionally, encourage students to discover more about the gospel by checking out the "Expedition: Supernova" section on page 16 of their *Mission Logs*.

CONTEMPLATING THE JOURNEY (optional)

To give students a quiet opportunity to connect with God, guide them through this contemplative prayer idea.

Have students find a spot away from others. If possible, dim the lights. Give each student a small cup of seeds or plastic pellets. Have students quietly run their fingers through the seeds while meditating on God's limitless plan for them. As there are many seeds in the cup, God has many loving plans for their lives.

Remind students to refer to page 15 of their *Mission Logs* for the Key Verse. Also make sure each student has a Bible available.

Expedition (45 minutes)

JOURNEY TO THE *OUTER LIMITS* – 10 minutes

Voyage number four...where are we going today?

Do the countdown together: **Five, four, three, two, one...**

Voyagers should now go to today's Expedition portion of their *Mission Logs* on page 16.

Our destination today is a Comet's Tail. Direct students to look at the information on and images of a comet's tail on the Expedition page.

The outer crust of comets is made up of ice, rock, and dust, although we don't know what's inside them.[8] As comets pass other planets, these planets have a strong impact on the comets, causing them to change paths, either sending them toward the Sun or out of the solar system into darkness.[9] As a comet travels near the Sun, the ice is melted and boils off, and a tail of gas and dust is created. We can see the tail, which always points toward the Sun, because the sun lights up the gas and dust particles.[10]

SNACK – 15 minutes

The Voyage 4 snack options are Peach Boats and Boats-a-float. Both of these nautical themed snacks serve as delicious representations of today's Bible story, reminding us that with God, all things are possible. If running *Outer Limits* simultaneously with the elementary *Cosmic City™* program, you may choose to gather all the children together for a large-group snack time. Otherwise, reference *The Shooting Star Drive-in Snack Guide* for specific instructions and recipes.

Experience (1 hour)

CRAFT: FLYING COMETS – 20 minutes

SUPPLIES
- ☐ Sample of completed craft
- ☐ Ripstop nylon fabric (1/2 yard for every three students)
- ☐ Dried beans or peas (1/2 cup per student)
- ☐ 1/2 cup measuring cup (at least one for every five students)
- ☐ Snack-sized plastic zip seal bags
- ☐ Sewing scissors (one pair per student)
- ☐ Measuring tape (for leader only)
- ☐ Rulers
- ☐ Markers (one per student)
- ☐ Yarn or sturdy string (approx. 12" per student)
- ☐ 3 hula hoops or masking tape (optional)

Voyage 4 Craft: Flying Comets

DO AHEAD
Cut 20 x 20-inch squares of the ripstop nylon fabric (one square per student). Cut 12-inch strands of yarn or sturdy string (one strand per student). Place supplies in neat piles on the craft table, making them easy for students to access.

QUICK TIP!
Play some fun, energetic background music as the students work on their craft project. Praise and worship music or contemporary Christian music will keep students moving along on their projects while enhancing the fun factor. You can also order copies of the *Cosmic City™ Praise Songs* CD, filled with original VBS-themed praise music, from www.cookvbs.com.

QUICK TIP!
The most time-intensive part of today's craft will be pre-cutting the fabric and string. As with earlier crafts, plan on coming early to do the cutting, and recruit a teen or adult volunteer to join you to make the process go much more quickly.

QUICK TIP!
As you go through the instructions, model each step and have students follow along.

QUICK TIP!
For today's voyage, your students will make their craft before playing the game, as the *Flying Comet* they create will be used in the game.

Today, you're going to make *Flying Comets*. My hope is that when you're finished, your comet will fly boldly through the air, serving as a reminder of God's perfect plan for your lives and the boldness you can have in him.

INSTRUCTIONS

1. Gather these supplies and bring them back to your seat: one fabric square, one string, one plastic snack bag, and one marker.
2. Fold your fabric square in half.
3. Tie your string tightly to the end of your marker. There should be about 9 inches of loose string.
4. Now hold down the loose end of the string at the midway point of the fold in your fabric.
5. Using the marker and string like a compass, draw a half circle; the folded edge should be at the top of the half circle.

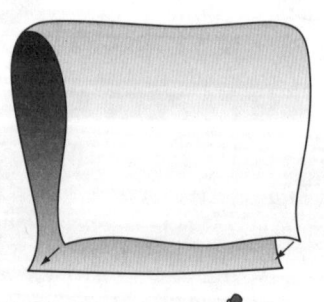

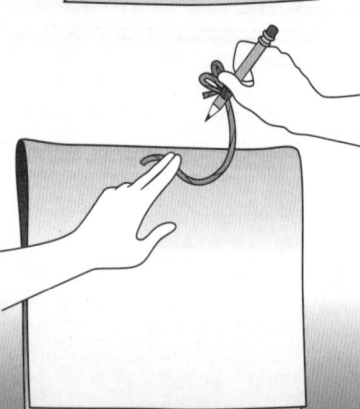

COSMIC CITY™ VBS Outer Limits Upper Elementary Guide

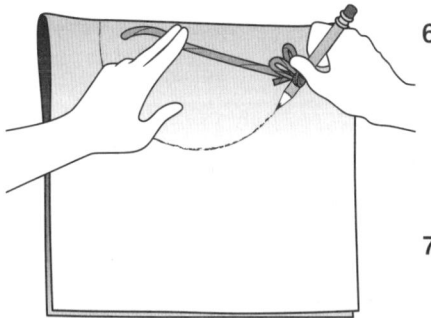

6. Keeping your fabric square folded in half, cut along the half-circle outline. When finished with this step, you will be able to unfold your fabric to have a full circle.
7. Fold your fabric circle into quarters. 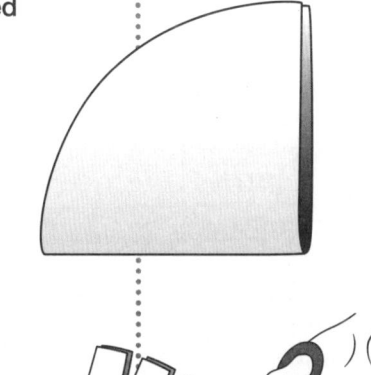
8. Keeping your fabric folded, cut slits along the outside of the circle to create the tail of your comet. Each slit should be about 5 inches deep and 1 inch wide.
9. Unfold the circle and lay it flat on the table. 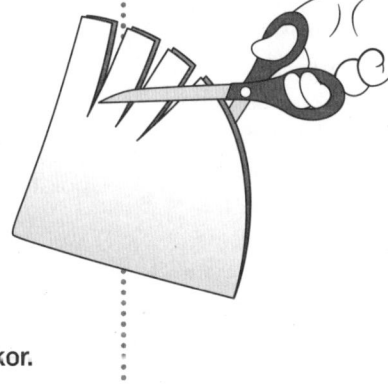
10. Now pour 1/2 cup of dried beans or peas into your snack-sized plastic bag. Tightly seal the bag.
11. Place the plastic bag, filled with dry beans or peas, in the center of the fabric circle. 
12. Remove your string from the marker.
13. Gather the ends of the circle together and tie your string tightly at the base of the strips.

Your comet is ready to fly!

GAME: RIDING A COMET'S TAIL — 20 minutes

Here's a game you can play using the comets from the craft. Have Space Voyagers get into the same Shuttle Teams from the previous activity. Have each team form a circle, and use one of the flying comets for each team. The first person throws it to someone else in the circle (not the person right next to him); this person throws to a third person, and so on until the bag comes back to the first person. Then, the Team must start over, in the exact same order. After a minute or two of this, call **Reverse!** and have students reverse the order exactly, without dropping the comet. After another minute, call **Reverse!** again, and students should resume the original order. Any time someone drops the comet or throws to the incorrect person, they must start the order over with the very first person. The goal is to get through six rounds.

After several minutes, tell students that for this next round, each time they catch the comet, they must sing one line of a song before throwing it to the next person. Expect a lot of laughter and some embarrassment during this round (but don't force students to sing; respect those who choose not to).

For the final round, say, **Mix it up!**, which means that students must rearrange the order of the circle (everyone must stand in a different spot). This time, throwing the comet in the same order will provide a bigger challenge, since people will be in different places.

Launch Farther!

To make an even stronger link to playing boldly, put blindfolds on each student for the last round, and tell them to start at the beginning one last time. They should see how many people they can get through. It'll be much more difficult because students will have to aim in each other's general direction, and reach out to catch the comet when they think it might be coming their way. Afterward, discuss what this experience was like, and how it's like the way we sometimes feel in life.

COSMIC CITY™ VBS Outer Limits Upper Elementary Guide

Launch Farther!

Create another fun, quick game that uses the *Flying Comets*. Designate a tossing line (masking tape works great if indoors and two cones or a stick if outside). Take three hula hoops (or if inside, use masking tape to create large circles on the floor) and place them in a line, each hoop several feet farther from the tossing line than the previous one. Assign a point value to each hoop (such as 10, 20, and 30 points), giving the highest value to the farthest hoop. Then have students take turns trying to toss their flying comets into the hoops. Each student gets three tosses; their scores are a culmination of all three. If implementing the week-long competition option, award points to the first, second, and third place students' Shuttle Teams.

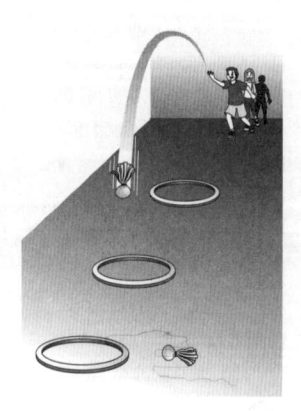

After completing the game, gather the large group together and discuss the following:

★ What kind of planning went into successfully completing a round?
★ How were you bold in this game? How were you *not* bold?
★ What does it mean to live boldly?
★ How does God's plan let you live boldly?

Like planets impacting a comet's path, you had these little comets going in many different directions. Yet there was still an order—even when you accidentally dropped them. God's wondrous plan has perfect order, even though sometimes it feels sort of chaotic. And God never drops us, so we can live boldly as we follow his plan.

Have students form Voyage Pairs, and as each person answers a question, have him or her toss the comet to his or her partner:

★ How will your comet remind you of God's wondrous plan?
★ What's one thing you'll do to practice living boldly?

Once all students have their own comets back, continue: **Comets are on such bold, unpredictable journeys; they speed along, burning up, vulnerable to being nudged off-course by the planets they pass. Yet they're lit up by the Sun, which is always behind them. Sounds familiar, doesn't it? Let's bring this home a little bit—at least to our solar system.**

LIVE IT! ACTIVITY – 25 minutes

Have students open their Mission Logs to page 17.

In your *Mission Logs* you'll see possible real-life scenarios. You may have even experienced some of these situations yourself. What I want you to do is practice how you'll respond in each scenario.

Have students form Shuttle Teams of four to six and discuss the scenarios, answering the question: **What would God want me to do, and why?**

For your reference, here are the scenarios found on page 17 in the *Mission Log*:

Scenario 1: You see another student being teased and bullied at school. If you stand up for him or her, they'll probably make fun of you too. What do you do?

Scenario 2: You're at the store with two of your friends. There are a lot of people standing all around you. Your friends tell you they're going to steal something *from the store, and dare you to do the same thing. If you don't, they'll laugh and tell everyone that you're a coward. What do you do?*

Scenario 3: One morning, you notice that your little brother is being a brat, your mom has a lot of work piled up around the house, and it looks like she's been crying. But it's a perfect summer day, and you have plans to make the best of it. What do you do?

Scenario 4: You're eating lunch with a group of people, including someone you've never met before. Within a few minutes, this person is saying that God doesn't exist, and anyone who believes in Jesus is an idiot. Everyone else seems to be agreeing, and you don't really want to cause any trouble. What do you do?

Scenario 5: Your friend calls you, crying. She tells you she just found out her parents are divorcing, and that her longtime pet has to be put to sleep. She asks you why God is letting all of this happen. What do you do?

After they've discussed every scenario, ask each Shuttle Team to plan out and then perform one scenario for everyone else; they should be sure to include the next step in the scenario, the "What do you do?" part. Give each team several minutes to prepare before performances begin. Afterward, lead the Mission Briefing in enthusiastic applause for everyone's performance.

Have students form groups of three or four to discuss these questions, found on page 17 in their *Mission Logs*:

★ How does practicing following Jesus, as you just did, help you become more bold?

★ What's the thing in your life that seems impossible, but you know is "possible with God"?

★ In what tangible way will you boldly follow God's plan for you this week?

Like comets, we too are on bold, unpredictable journeys. It often feels like we're going to crash, burn, or get pushed off into infinite space. But when we're in a relationship with Jesus, the true "Son," he lights us up as we point toward him. So we can continue flying along boldly because we know God's plans for us are wonderful and have no limits. Now encourage students to spend the next few minutes completing the prayer at the bottom of page 17 in their *Mission Logs*.

QUICK TIP!

All students may not be needed to act in every scenario. However, encourage everyone to find a role, such as director, prop, or even background scenery. This will give the shier students something important to do without embarrassing them.

Launch Farther!

Since tomorrow is the last day of the program, you may want to have a party. Ask students to help you plan the celebration, and include the Voyagers' families, good food, more games (maybe the favorites from the week), show-and-tell of all the crafts, and lots of storytelling. Have volunteers write what food they'll bring on a sign-up sheet, and remind students to bring all the crafts they've created throughout the week.

You may even want to create an invitation that students can give their parents, inviting them to join in the festivities during the last 30 minutes of tomorrow's program. Or you can download the customizable invitation available on the *Cosmic City*™ VBS CD-ROM.

CLOSING ASSEMBLY – 15 minutes

I know you've been wondering what's happening to the heroes from our drama this morning. Let's go warp speed right back into the action...

Actors perform the skit for Voyage 4: Part 2. The script for today's skit can be found on pages 106–107 of this guide.

Tour Host gives announcements. Be sure to include any specific additional information.

Tomorrow we'll visit our final destination, and discover one more of God's amazing wonders. Don't miss it—be here at [program's start time], and bring your money for the mission project. Also, take home today's *Mission Log* pages and experience the activities with your family. You'll also choose which Cosmic Challenges you'll embark on before we meet again. Be sure to wear comfortable clothes so that you'll be able to easily move around and do a craft.

We have to take off like comets now, but get ready for another exciting expedition tomorrow. See you then!

Notes

Notes

VOYAGE 5

The Wonder of God Brought Down to Earth

BIBLE STORY
Jesus' Resurrection (John 19:1–6, 16–18; 20:1–8)

KEY VERSE
I want to know Christ and the power of his resurrection. (Phil. 3:10)

LIVE IT!
God's wondrous grace has no limits! I can spread his good news to others.

Exploration (1 hour, 15 minutes)

OPENING ASSEMBLY – 30 minutes

Outer Limits Leader welcomes students.
Welcome to the last Voyage to the *Outer Limits*! You're about to visit our final destination and encounter what is definitely God's greatest wonder. So, hold on for dear life and savor every moment, starting with a glimpse into what our favorite space heroes are up to...

Actors perform the skit for Voyage 5: Part 1. The script for today's skit can be found on pages 108–110 of this guide.

Outer Limits Leader or another adult gives an update on the daily mission project.

Share the Wonder: There—Bibles for Brazil

It's our final day collecting money to send books about Jesus to Brazil. Hold up sample book. **You all have done a great job this week. If anyone brought change today, we'll collect it now. As we do that, I want to thank you for all you've done so far. These books really mean a lot to the people in Pernambuco. A leader of one of the churches there has received a few of the books in the past. He said that many people in his area are accepting Jesus as their Savior and**

COSMIC CITY™ VBS Outer Limits Upper Elementary Guide

QUICK TIP!
You may want to give information about the celebration that'll happen during today's Closing Assembly, and ask students to set the crafts they've brought in a particular place, where they'll be safe for the next few hours.

QUICK TIP!
Write the following questions on a whiteboard or large poster for students to use as a prompt in discussion with their partner. If you've been using the same poster each day, be sure to update the Key Verse to Philippians 3:10.
- Which challenge or challenges from yesterday's "Back to Earth" page did you do?
- What did you learn about yourself from completing it? About others? About God?
- With your partner, say yesterday's Key Verse (Mark 10:27) to each other. If you need a little help reviewing, look it up in the Bible as you read it together.

really want to know about God and follow him. But the leaders of the church have no Bibles to give them. Not long ago, the church leaders were praying that God would send them Bibles, books, and other things to help. Then they heard about the chance to receive books like the ones we're sending and praised God for hearing their prayers. The books arrived sooner than they thought. They thanked God for the books with a special worship service and gave them to the very poorest people, even though no one had very much for themselves. As you can tell by what this leader said, what you kids have done this week is going to make a big difference in people's lives. At our closing assembly today, I'll let you know how many books we're sending. Just wait until you hear—you have all done an incredible job! Thanks for giving so much!

Tour Host gives announcements, including any additional information specific to your program.

You've done such a terrific job in each Voyage; we know you'll do the same today.

Have students meet in Voyager Pairs for challenge check-in. Give students one or two minutes to tell their partners which challenges from their "Back to Earth" page they accomplished, and what they learned from it—about themselves, others, or God. When finished sharing, have each pair say yesterday's Key Verse (Mark 10:27) to each other. If they struggle saying it from memory, ask them to look it up in the Bible and review it together.

Tour Director, Tour Host, or teen Guide prays:

Father, we've loved spending this time with you and each other; thank you for a week of learning more about who you are. Help us to respond to your plans by boldly following Jesus. Be with us on our last Voyage today. We love you. In Jesus' name, amen.

Worship Blastoff

A leader plays the *Cosmic City*™ theme song. You can choose to play the *Cosmic City*™ *Music and Promo* DVD with guided motions, have students create their own movements to accompany the song, or do the following: **Let's sing our theme song one last time! And pump this song up by putting together everything we've done. While you're singing the verses, snap your fingers and turn around. When you're singing the chorus, stomp your feet and clap your hands.**

Rally *(optional)* – 15 minutes

If you choose this option, you'll play the *Cosmic City*™ *Praise Songs* CD or *Cosmic City*™ *Music and Promo* DVD for portions of this time and have a live worship band lead other parts.

God deserves our most sincere worship. Pour your gratitude and love into these songs as we praise God for being our Lord, Savior, and Friend.

Song suggestions:
* *God of Power* (Phil Reynolds, *Cosmic City*™ VBS *Praise Songs* CD and *Cosmic City*™ VBS *Music and Promo* DVD)
* *Master of the Universe* (Kathy Ulrich, *Cosmic City*™ VBS *Praise Songs* CD and *Cosmic City*™ VBS *Music and Promo* DVD)
* *Amazing Grace* (John Newton)
* *Breathe* (Marie Barnett)
* *Come Thou Fount of Every Blessing* (John Wyeth)
* *Shine, Jesus, Shine* (Graham Kendrick)

You may read the following passages aloud in between songs, have a volunteer read the verses aloud, or say the Scriptures together: Romans 6:4 and John 3:16.

BIBLE STORY/KEY VERSE/LIVE IT! – 30 minutes

Space Voyagers, form Shuttle Teams of two to four people. You're going to read John 19:1-6, 16-18, and 20:1-8 as a team (these Scriptures are listed on page 19 of your *Mission Logs*). Then as a group read the Bible story summary on the same *Mission Log* page. Finally, work together to create a visual version of the story.

Direct everyone to page 19 in their *Mission Logs* and hand out a blank sheet of printer paper to each student. Then have each team draw images from today's Bible story in three or four separate frames. Tell students that these should look like storyboards or comics, although they don't have to be funny. Also tell students that the images they draw don't have to be literal, capturing all the characters and plot points. Instead, they might choose only single images or icons to reflect the meaning of the Scripture (for instance, a cross, a tear, or an exclamation point). Students can refer to the story summary on page 19 of their *Mission Logs* for help.

Ask teams to call out "Stellar!" when they've finished with their storyboards. Then have students discuss the following questions with their group. (These questions can be found on page 21 in their *Mission Logs*.)

* What was it like to capture this story through visual images?
* If you had to circle one frame of your storyboard as the most important, which would it be and why?

QUICK TIP!
Be a little more flexible on this final day; take some time to publicly thank all your volunteers and other leaders for their hard work. Also, give students the opportunity to express their thanks and thoughts about the program. This'll bring closure to one wonderful experience, and will also help you improve those experiences yet to follow.

Launch Farther!

If you're using the competition option, have students form those teams for this activity, and go forward as directed.

QUICK TIP!
Even though each student will have a storyboard frame in his or her *Mission Log*, have each group create a final version to share. The others can be duplicates of what the group draws, or be used to brainstorm initial ideas. Have sheets of blank paper available so students can create their final group version apart from their Mission Logs.

Also, to prevent certain students from dominating the drawing process, make sure that everyone has a chance to contribute to at least one frame. Suggest that the more skilled or enthusiastic artists help guide the overall vision of the project.

QUICK TIP!

You may want to explain what the Key Verse means to you—understanding that God sent his Son, Jesus, to Earth, to die on the cross, taking on the punishment for everyone's sins. Jesus Christ then rose from the dead three days later. Death has no power over you either, because you've accepted that Jesus died for your sins and you'll have eternal life, being with God forever.

QUICK TIP!

As you talk about a relationship with Jesus, be sure that these things are on your heart and mind:

- Focus on the true meaning of the gospel.
- Help Christian students articulate their faith, and give them an opportunity to renew their intimacy with Christ.
- Encourage other students to ask questions and give them an opportunity to know Christ for perhaps the first time.
- Ask God to lead you in the appropriate way through each of these valuable discussions.
- For ideas on helping invite students to Christ, see page 26 of this guide.

★ What do you think it means to "know Christ and the power of his resurrection"?

★ What does knowing Christ and the power of his resurrection mean to you? How might it change the way you live your life at home? At school?

★ What's the difference between knowing someone and knowing "about" them? Give an example of knowing something "about" Jesus, but not really knowing him personally?

Have everyone say today's "**Live It!**" together, reading from the top of page 19 in their *Mission Logs*: **"God's wondrous grace has no limits! I can spread his good news to others."** Then ask:

★ How would you express the good news to someone who doesn't know about Jesus? to a friend? a family member?

You did a great job expressing the good news through pictures. God sent his Son, Jesus, to die for our sins, and then be resurrected so that we might be forgiven and live with God forever in heaven. Before Jesus, God wanted people to offer physical sacrifices, such as an animal, to be right with him. But Jesus became the sacrifice for all time, so people no longer have to do what they did before. They just have to know and personally accept that Jesus took on death and defeated it, rising again so that we might all live forever with God in heaven. Now that is good news we can share with others!

Continue this discussion with the whole group, allowing space for students to teach and learn from each other:

★ What does Jesus' sacrifice mean to you? What does it mean to be in a relationship with Jesus? How does someone have a relationship with Jesus?

★ How would you describe your own relationship with Jesus? How do you want it to change, if at all?

God resurrected Jesus from the dead, destroying sin's power over any of us. We can experience a close, intimate relationship with Jesus. All it takes is acknowledging what Jesus did for us, and inviting him into our lives.

Say the following prayer, pausing for students to repeat after you, either silently or aloud.

Jesus, thank you so much for dying on the cross and rising again, so that my sins are forgiven and I can have eternal life with you in heaven. Please enter my life and, by your power, help me not to sin—but instead trust and obey you. Thank you for loving me so much that I can be in a relationship with you. In Jesus' name, amen.

CONTEMPLATING THE JOURNEY (optional)

To give students a quiet opportunity to connect with God, guide them through this idea for prayerfully contemplating Philippians 3:10.

Have students find a spot away from others. If possible, dim the lights. Give each student an index card and pencil, and have them write an intimate prayer to God about what Jesus' resurrection means to them. Tell students that this should be a love letter to God, thanking him and being as honest with him as they can.

Remind students to refer to page 19 in their *Mission Logs* for the Key Verse. You can also make sure each student has a Bible available.

Expedition (45 minutes)

JOURNEY TO THE *OUTER LIMITS* – 10 minutes

It's time for one last countdown to one last destination: Five, four, three, two, one…

Voyagers should go to today's Expedition section on page 21 of their *Mission Logs*.

Our destination today is the edge of a black hole. Direct students to look at the information and images on black holes on the Expedition page. Then discuss the questions below as a whole-group Mission Briefing.

I know, you're probably thinking: *that's it, that's our last destination? That's not a big deal at all!* Well, it's a lot cooler than you may think. The area around a black hole doesn't let matter pass, and instead pulls it into the hole.[11] In fact, several suns can be pulled in and held in a black hole at one time. Except a black hole isn't really a hole: it could look like everything from a sphere, to a ring, to a spinning top.[12] When matter's pulled into these massive rings in space, it causes brilliant displays of light.[13] And, did you know that a black hole or ring is always in the center of its galaxy? Once something's pulled in, it's there forever, and never comes out.[14] Finally, you can't actually see a black hole. The only way you can tell its location is by those light displays—rays of light bending and refracting all around the black hole.[15]

Discuss with students:

★ **How's a black hole or ring like or unlike God?** (You may need to help students a bit to make this abstract connection. For example, explain that just as a black hole pulls things into it, causing brilliant displays of light, God calls us to him. And when we join him in relationship, his brilliant light is reflected in us.)

★ Wow, the edge of a black hole is a pretty powerful place! In what ways might we act like one in other people's lives?

So, let's explore what this has to do with God through a game called "Living on the Edge."

GAME: LIVING ON THE EDGE — 20 minutes

Ahead of time, write random character roles on slips of paper, at least one for each student. These roles can include: dog, teacher, police officer, cartoon character, mouse, famous actor, doctor, and so on. Tape each paper to a Voyager's back without letting him or her see it.

Each of you has a different, and unique, character taped to your back. Try to find out who you are by walking around and interacting with other Voyagers. No one can tell you directly what or who you are, but you can ask them yes or no questions. Each person can ask eight questions total; after that, he or she must guess correctly or sit out. You're responsible for keeping track of how many questions you've asked and sitting out if you reach eight without correctly guessing your character—we're on the honor system.

Allow students to mingle and ask each other yes or no questions until everyone is out, or a sufficient amount of time has passed.

Discuss as a Mission Briefing:
★ What was it like to try to guess who you were?
★ What was it like trying to help others guess their characters?
★ How is this like or unlike our "Live It!" for today? (God's wondrous grace has no limits! I can spread his good news to others.)

What you did in this game is kind of like spreading the good news; you helped people to know who they really are. Now, there are some major differences: being a dog or a mouse is not the same thing as being someone very precious whom God created, loves, and died for. And we can definitely use more than "yes" or "no" to tell others, which is really great news!

SNACK – 15 minutes

Today's snack options are Berry Blastoffs, a space-themed fruit treat, and Resurrection Butterflies, a tasty reminder that we are new creations in Christ. If running *Outer Limits* simultaneously with the elementary *Cosmic City*™ program, you may choose to gather all the children together for a large-group snack time. Otherwise, reference *The Shooting Star Drive-in Snack Guide* for specific instructions and recipes.

Experience (1 hour)

CRAFT: BUTTERFLY BACKPACK DANGLERS – 20 minutes

Launch Farther!

You may choose to use the alternate Voyage 5 craft option, *One-of-a-Kind Keychains*, as a supplement or substitute for the Butterfly Backpack Danglers. Details are provided on page 85.

SUPPLIES
- ☐ Sample of completed craft
- ☐ Various colors of felt (i.e. white, green, pink, purple, red, black, orange) (approx. one 8.5" x 11" piece for every two students)
- ☐ Photocopies of the *Butterfly Backpack Dangler* pattern found on page 87 of this Leader's Guide (one pattern per student)
- ☐ 6 mm googly eyes (two eyes per student)
- ☐ Small ball chains (to use for attaching to backpack) (one per student)
- ☐ Yarn (approx. 6" per student)
- ☐ Rulers
- ☐ Scissors
- ☐ Single hole punch
- ☐ Felt glue
- ☐ Pencils
- ☐ Glitter glue and/or puff paint (optional)
- ☐ Small gift bags and tissue paper (optional)

Voyage 5 Craft: Butterfly Backpack Danglers

DO AHEAD
Make photocopies of the *Butterfly Backpack Dangler* pattern found on page 87 of this guide (one copy of pattern per student). Lay out all other supplies in neat piles on the craft table, making them easy for students to access.

Just as each black hole is the center of its galaxy, God is the Center—of everything. We can pull others toward him, and share the good news about his grace and forgiveness. Today you're going to create a gift, a gift that represents the good news of Christ's death and resurrection. A gift that you're going to give freely to a friend or family member, just as Jesus freely gives each of us the gift of eternal life.

COSMIC CITY™ VBS Outer Limits Upper Elementary Guide *81*

Launch Farther!

If time allows, have additional decorating supplies available to students, such as glitter glue and puff paints. Allow students to personalize their butterflies through adding individual decorative touches. Just be cognizant of how long it takes various glues and paints to dry, and take this into account when planning.

The gift that you'll be creating is called a *Butterfly Backpack Dangler*. Now butterflies don't live a typical life. They go through an incredible transformation, changing from one thing into something totally new. **Who can tell us about this transformation that butterflies go through?** Allow a student to explain the change that butterflies undergo, from caterpillar, to cocoon, to beautiful and colorful butterfly.

Because Jesus died for our sins and then rose again, we, like butterflies, can become new creations. The Bible describes this process in 2 Corinthians 5:17: "Therefore, if anyone is in Christ, he is a new creation; the old has gone, the new has come!"

So let's get started on making our gifts.

INSTRUCTIONS

1. Carefully cut out the three pieces of your Butterfly Backpack Dangler pattern.
2. One at a time, trace each pattern piece onto a different color felt. (One color for one wing piece, another for the next wing piece, a third for the final wing piece, and a final color for the body.) Be careful to trace along the edges of the felt and not in the middle so that there is plenty of felt left for other students to use.
3. Cut out the felt along your traced lines.
4. Cut two 3-inch pieces of yarn and tie a knot at one end of each. These will become your butterfly's antennae.
5. Now lay out your butterfly, layering each felt piece as you see it in the sample craft.
6. Place two googly eyes on your butterfly's head and the antennae at the top.
7. Once your butterfly is laid out as you like, begin gluing together the pieces. Start with the wing bottom piece, then the smaller middle wing piece, then the top wing piece, and finally the body. Finish by gluing on the eyes and the two yarn antennae. (You will actually glue the un-knotted ends of the antennae to the backside of the head.)
8. Using the hole punch, make a hole in the top part of the butterfly's wing.
9. String a ball chain through the hole, completing your *Butterfly Backpack Dangler*.

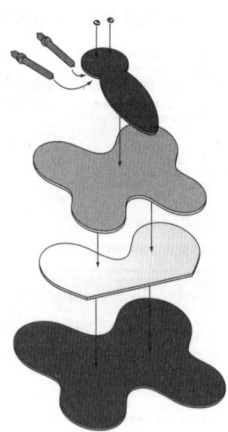

Launch Farther!

Because students will be giving their *Butterfly Backpack Danglers* away as gifts, provide small gift bags and tissue paper. Then encourage students to neatly wrap their crafts, so they're ready to give away.

Have students form Voyage Pairs and discuss the following questions:

★ How will your butterfly remind you of the good news of Jesus?
★ Pretend that you're giving your *Butterfly Backpack Dangler* to

your partner as a gift. What would you say to her so that she understands what the butterfly symbolizes? (Be sure to talk about Jesus, his death and resurrection, and our opportunity to become new creatures who know God personally and will live forever.)

Once all pairs are finished discussing, continue: **When you leave *Outer Limits* today, I don't want you to toss your butterfly under your bed or in a drawer. Instead, I challenge you to give it as a gift to a friend or family member who may not know the good news of Jesus. As you give the gift, explain what Jesus did for each of us on the cross and how the butterfly can be a constant reminder of this great news! Your friend can put it on his backpack, keychain, or even a doorknob.**

LIVE IT! ACTIVITY – 25 minutes

During the next few minutes, you're going to get a chance to create a "Good News Board"—a collage that represents who Jesus is to you and the good news that he offers to everyone. Keep in mind that you're not creating a Good News Board so that you can keep it to yourself, hidden in a place where no other eyes will see it. You're creating a board to hang in a place where friends or family will see it every day, a place where others will see and learn about the love of Jesus.

So what's a Good News Board? Let's find out . . .

Distribute family-friendly magazines that are full of interesting images (one or two for each student), and have students open their *Mission Logs* to page 20. Then hand out sheets of 8.5 x 11-inch tag board (one for each student).

From both the *Mission Logs* and magazines, have students cut or tear out quotes, words, and images that could help bring someone they know into a relationship with Jesus.

Once everyone has several images and words from both page 20 of the *Mission Logs* and the magazines, have Space Voyagers tape or glue these things to their tag board while sharing why they chose them.

Have students discuss these questions with someone in the group who they haven't yet talked to today, referring to page 20 in their *Mission Logs* where the questions are listed:

★ **How will your Good News Board remind you of what it means to "know Christ and the power of his resurrection"?**

★ **Where will you put this board as a way of sharing about Jesus with others? (On your locker door, inside your desk at school, on your bedroom door, etc.)**

★ **You plan on giving away your butterfly as a gift and posting your Good**

QUICK TIP!

You might want to take a few moments before this activity to brainstorm ideas with your students. Talk about what images could represent a relationship with Jesus— sharing the good news with someone. For instance, words such as "love," or "sacrifice," or "hero;" pictures of a cross, crown, or baby. Students may also choose more general symbolic images, such as the color red, a tree, water, or a light bulb. Encourage students to be creative and think outside the literal box during this experience. For instance, how might an ad for shoes, a picture of a football star, or a brand-name soda represent a relationship with Jesus?

Launch Farther!

Today's Closing
Assembly will be different from the rest; since it's the final day, you'll celebrate with the students and their parents, who have also been invited. Have volunteers run the games from the week (choose the two or three that were most popular), and set out food for everyone to enjoy (pizza, deli sandwiches, or just snacks will work well). Students should have all of their crafts to show off. Ask students to tell stories from the week, including the funniest and most exciting thing that happened. End your party by praying together that God will continue helping you explore the *Outer Limits* of a relationship with him.

News Board in a place where many others will see it. What are some other ways you can commit to spreading the good news?

Have Shuttle Teams of two or three meet together and pray over these boards and the people who will see them.

God's wondrous grace has no limits. We can all spread his good news to others. Jesus truly is the Wonder of God brought down to Earth. We've had some pretty incredible expeditions and learned lots of extraordinary things about space. But in all the galaxy, the most extraordinary, incredible thing that's ever happened is Jesus coming to Earth, dying, and coming back to life, so that each of us can have eternal life and a personal friendship with him.

Have students refer to page 19 in their *Mission Logs* and say aloud the Key Verse together: **"I want to know Christ and the power of his resurrection (Phil. 3:10)."** Encourage students to review this verse as they go to bed tonight and again when they wake up the next morning. This may be the end of their visit to the *Outer Limits*, but it's surely not the end of their journey in knowing God.

CLOSING ASSEMBLY – 15 minutes
And now, here's the last of the dramas from The Outer Limits Theater Group. Enjoy!

Actors perform the skit for Voyage 5: Part 2. The script for today's skit can be found on page 111 of this guide.

Tour Host gives announcements, welcomes parents to the closing festivities, and includes any additional information specific to your program.

Please stay and clean up if you're able to. Also, take home the rest of your *Mission Log*, and experience the activities with your family. You'll also choose your Cosmic Challenges, but since we won't be meeting to check in, be sure to tell someone what you accomplished. Be sure to announce the final number of Bibles that children in Brazil will receive because of the money raised during *Outer Limits* ($1 equals two Bibles).

You've been the best Space Voyagers who've ever explored the universe! Thanks for joining us on this extreme, stellar expedition.

Launch Farther! The *Outer Limits* experience doesn't end today. Set a follow-up plan in motion now. Write or call each participant's family to get feedback about the program, and ask your volunteers for their insights. Meet with your leadership team to pray that God will continue to work in the hearts and minds of the students who were involved in the program.

At www.cookvbs.com, you can find creative thematic photo frames. Take photos of each student, Shuttle Team, or the large group sometime during this final Voyage. Put a photo from the week in the picture frame and hand them to each student as she leaves. Or you can mail the frames to each student next week as a follow-up.

If you have any extra food or supplies from the week, consider giving it to families in need (ask your pastor for ideas). Send thank-you notes to the church leaders and volunteers who've helped you throughout the program.

Voyage 5 Alternate Craft: One-of-a-Kind Keychain

SUPPLIES
- [ ] Sample of completed craft
- [ ] Various colors of felt
- [ ] Small ball chains (one per student)
- [ ] Rulers
- [ ] Scissors
- [ ] Single hole punch
- [ ] Felt glue
- [ ] Pencils
- [ ] Glitter glue and/or puff paint (optional)

DO AHEAD
Create your own unique felt keychain. Lay out supplies in neat piles on the craft table, making them easy for students to access.

Similar to the *Butterfly Backpack Danglers*, students can make *One-of-a-Kind Keychains* to give as gifts to friends or family members. The same supplies are used for both crafts, so you may choose to give students the option of completing either craft.

INSTRUCTIONS

1. Cut three to seven various shapes from different colors of felt. (Each shape should be no larger than your hand.) These shapes can be geometric shapes you're familiar with, such as squares, triangles, and circles. Or they can be unique abstract shapes that you've never seen before. Try choosing colors and shapes that are meaningful to you. For example, perhaps you love to run in the green grass that God created, so you cut a jagged grass-like shape out of green felt.

2. Arrange your felt shapes so they overlap, one on top of the other, to form a collage of meaningful shapes and colors.

COSMIC CITY™ VBS Outer Limits Upper Elementary Guide

3. Begin gluing together your felt pieces. Start with the bottom piece and glue each piece to the one directly on top of it.
4. Using the hole punch, make a hole in the top part of your *One-of-a-Kind Keychain*.
5. String a ball chain through the hole, completing your *One-of-a-Kind Keychain*.

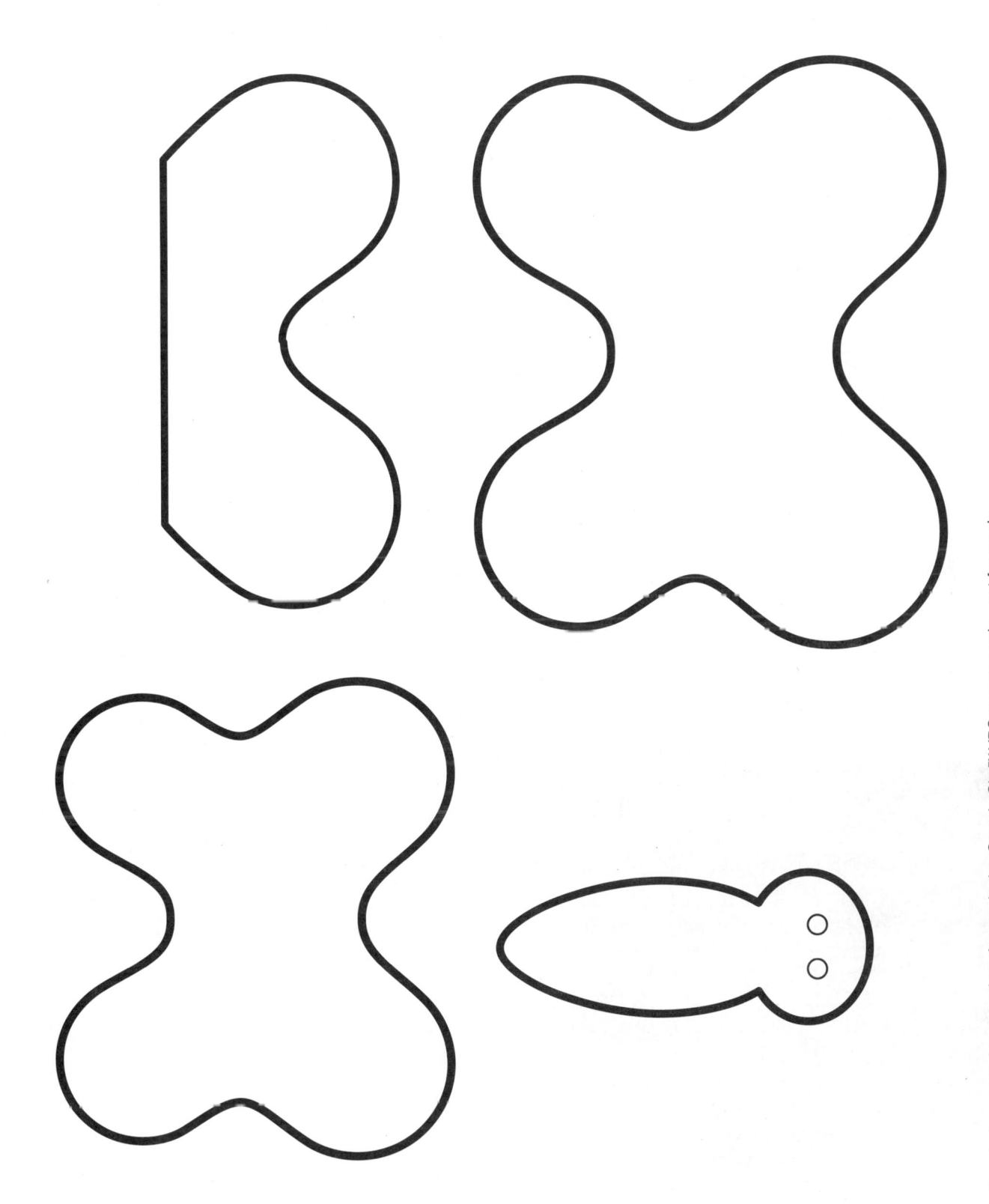

COSMIC CITY™ VBS Outer Limits Upper Elementary Guide *87*

Notes

Skit Scripts

Voyage 1: Part 1

CAST: Teen 1, Teen 2, Robot
PROPS: boxes, silver paint, 2 watches, stage lights
SET-UP: The Robot could be a teen with silver-painted boxes on his head and trunk. The box around the waist needs to be square like an oven, and the box on the head can have eyeholes cut out of it. The two teen characters should dress modestly as typical American teenagers (i.e. t-shirt, jeans, and sneakers or flip-flops).
SCENE: Teen 1 and Teen 2 run onstage.

TEEN 2: Wait! Stop! I can't run any farther.
TEEN 1: We have to keep going. There's an angry Piedron after us.
TEEN 2: I don't care. I'm too tired to move another step. *(Teen 1 stops.)*
TEEN 1: Do you know what a Piedron will do to you if it catches you?
TEEN 2: No.
TEEN 1: Neither do I, and I don't want to find out.
TEEN 2: We've been running from it for days. We can't go on like this.
TEEN 1: I guess we can stop for a couple of milliseconds.
TEEN 2: Thank you. Do you have any idea where we can go to get away from the Piedron?
TEEN 1: I didn't think it would find us here.
TEEN 2: This place looks scarier than the last.
TEEN 1: The last planet had poisonous gases on it!
TEEN 2: You're right, but that wasn't scary. We just couldn't breathe. The black hole was a little scary, especially when we almost got sucked into it.
TEEN 1: It was night. I couldn't tell the difference between it and the darkness.
TEEN 2: I didn't like being bombarded by asteroids either.
TEEN 1: Good thing we had our vapor shields with us then.
TEEN 2: You're missing the point.
TEEN 1: Which is? *(Robot enters and slowly moves toward them. His movements are stiff and mechanical. His words are pronounced individually, like those found on an answering machine.)*

QUICK TIP!
The robot character is unusually fond of pies (yum, yum). Pronounce his name "Pie-dron" to reflect this fondness.

TEEN 2: Piedron!

TEEN 1: I know, it's after us, but what's your point?

TEEN 2: No. Piedron! *(Points)*

ROBOT: Come with me. Resistance is futile.

TEEN 1: Oh no! It's cut off our escape.

TEEN 2: What're we going to do?

ROBOT: Come with me. Resistance is futile.

TEEN 1: I have an idea.

TEEN 2: It better be good. Getting lost in the Milky Way was not as fun as it sounded. I thought I'd get stuck between large cookies and larger glasses of milk.

TEEN 1: No. It's nothing like that. Set the coordinates on your time band to 001.

TEEN 2: But—

ROBOT: Come with me. Resistance is futile.

TEEN 2: Now! *(Teen 1 and Teen 2 press a button on their watches. They drop to a crouching position. The Robot moves backward until it's offstage. Most of the lights in the room and onstage should go off. Teen 1 and Teen 2 stand.)*

TEEN 2: Where are we?

TEEN 1: The only place I know where Piedrons don't exist.

TEEN 2: It's so dark here. Is it night?

TEEN 1: No. I don't think so. Well maybe. But I don't think night's been invented yet.

TEEN 2: What do you mean?

TEEN 1: You don't see a Piedron, do you?

TEEN 2: No.

TEEN 1: Then it doesn't matter whether it's day or night.

TEEN 2: It's so dark though. I can't see anything. Just because I can't see one doesn't mean there isn't one here. Piedrons have been around a long time. People made them thousands of years ago. We'd have to be at the creation of the universe to know we were safe from them.

TEEN 1: That's where we are.

TEEN 2: What? We're at the creation of the universe?

TEEN 1: Yeah.

TEEN 2: Where exactly?

TEEN 1: Around planet Earth, I think.

TEEN 2: There's nothing here. Not even stars. It's so dark I can't even see you. Where are you?

TEEN 1: I'm right here. It is dark, but that's because there's not even anything here. It's a void. If Earth had been created, it would've been right here. But if the Earth hasn't been created, then Piedrons haven't been invented either.

QUICK TIP!

If the actors haven't memorized the script, a reading light will be needed when the lights are turned off. Consider using small flashlights or a music stand with light attached.

TEEN 2: True. There's nothing here to make anything with. What did God use to make the universe? I don't see anything he could mix together to make stuff.

TEEN 1: You're right. There's nothing here. God made the whole universe—suns, stars, planets, asteroids, everything—out of nothing.

TEEN 2: Wow. That's amazing. *(Pause)* I don't like this place. Let's get out of here. I'd rather face a Piedron than be stuck in all this nothingness.

TEEN 1: Okay, set coordinates to 477.

TEEN 2: I can't see the coordinates on my watch.

TEEN 1: Neither can I.

TEEN 2: Without being able to set coordinates, we won't be able to leave.

TEEN 1: You're right, again.

TEEN 2: What should we do?

TEEN 1: I have no idea.

TEEN 2: I want out of here.

TEEN 1: Me too.

TEEN 2: If we can't leave, it means we're stuck here.

TEEN 1: Yeah.

TEEN 2: We're stuck here?

TEEN 1: I think so.

TEEN 2: Oh no, we'll never get out of here!

TEEN 1: Let's not panic.

TEEN 2: I don't know about you, but I don't know what else to do. Help! Help! Someone help us!

TEEN 1: Who's going to hear you? There's nothing here.

TEEN 2: I don't know. Help! Is anyone there? Help!

TEEN 1: Help! *(Teen 1 and Teen 2 should both be yelling "help" to end the opening segment of this skit.)*

Voyage 1: Part 2

CAST: Teen 1, Teen 2, Robot
PROPS: 2 watches, microphone
SET-UP: Classroom lights should be turned off. Microphone should be backstage.
SCENE: Teen 1 and Teen 2 are onstage yelling for help. Both are wearing watches.

TEEN 2: Help! Help!

TEEN 1: Help!

TEEN 2: We're stuck here forever. We're stuck in a nothing void.

TEEN 1: Yelling is not going to get us anywhere.

TEEN 2: But I'm going to keep yelling. *(Before Teen 2 can open his mouth to yell again, a deep voice backstage says, "Let there be light." Someone should turn on the classroom and stage lights.)*

TEEN 1: Wow!

TEEN 2: Get us out of here. What are the coordinates? I know, 392. *(Teen 2 punches numbers in his time band and drops down to a crouching position.)*

TEEN 1: No! That won't take us back. I guess I'll have to go after him. *(Teen 1 punches in the same coordinates, drops down to a crouching position as Teen 2 stands. Within seconds, Teen 1 stands, also.)*

TEEN 2: Where are we now?

TEEN 1: You typed in the coordinates for a zoo on the planet Earth, hundreds of years ago.

TEEN 2: A zoo? A real zoo? Can I feed the elephants? I've always wanted to do that.

TEEN 1: No. They have signs all over saying not to feed the animals.

TEEN 2: Oh. Oh well. This is a pretty amazing place anyway. We went from nothing to all of this.

TEEN 1: Yeah. From nothing, God made each of these animals. He came up with a different idea for each one.

TEEN 2: That's a lot of work. None of them are the same.

TEEN 1: God is really creative.

TEEN 2: Let's go back to our time period.

TEEN 1: Set coordinates for 477. *(Teen 1 and Teen 2 punch the numbers on their time bands and crouch before standing.)*

TEEN 2: Yeah! We're back!

TEEN 1: Back amid the planets, stars, and other amazing things God created.

TEEN 2: And people. Look at all those people. *(Points to kids in the audience.)*

TEEN 1: God made each person in this room unique and special. Even twins are different, although you sometimes have to look close to find those differences.

TEEN 2: God's creativity has no limits!

TEEN 1: And you can experience his handiwork wherever you go.
TEEN 2: Let's get back to our spaceship and experience it there.
TEEN 1: Why not here? *(The Piedron enters again.)*
TEEN 2: I can think of one good reason. *(Points)*
ROBOT: Come with me. Resistance is futile.
TEEN 1: Good idea. God's wondrous creativity has no limits. Let's definitely experience it somewhere else! *(Teen 1 and Teen 2 run offstage, followed by the Piedron.)*

Voyage 2: Part 1

CAST: Teen 1, Teen 2, Robot

PROPS: card table, gray blanket, boxes, paint, rope, cardboard, apples, carrots, corn, spaceship

SET-UP: The spaceship can be made from a flat sheet of cardboard (or cardboard taped together) with rope handles on the wrong side. There should be two windows in the spaceship so teens can be seen through the windows. There should be a large rock onstage. This can be made out of a card table with a gray blanket over it. Apples, carrots, and corn should be placed on top of the rock.

SCENE: Teen 1 and 2 enter riding in the spaceship.

TEEN 2: I'm so hungry.

TEEN 1: Me too.

TEEN 2: We've been running from that Piedron for days. We have to stop somewhere for food.

TEEN 1: What about down there? *(Points)* My instruments say air and plants are down there.

TEEN 2: And even better, it's an uncharted planet. No Piedron should find us here.

TEEN 1: Let's land.

(Teen 1 and 2 should fly around the stage and then set down the cardboard spaceship as if they're landing. As they get out of the ship, the spaceship can lie flat on the stage.)

TEEN 2: What's that smell?

TEEN 1: Apples. They must have apple trees here, maybe a whole orchard. Apples are my favorite fruit in the whole world.

TEEN 2: I smell apples too, but I also smell something else. Is it corn or carrots? I can't tell. Those are vegetable smells. I love vegetables more than any other food.

TEEN 1: Let's find them.

TEEN 2: Lead the way.

(Teen 1 and 2 move toward a large rock. A Robot suddenly comes from behind the rock. The Robot's movements are stiff and mechanical. His words are pronounced individually, like those found on an answering machine.)

ROBOT: Come with me. Resistance is futile.

TEEN 1: It's a Piedron!

TEEN 2: Let's get out of here!

(They run from the Piedron and end up on the other side of the rock.)

ROBOT: Come with me. Resistance is futile.

TEEN 1: We can't go back to the ship without food!

TEEN 2: We have to.

TEEN 1: Not without a few apples.
TEEN 2: Forget the apples. Run!
(Teen 1 reaches for an apple, but the Piedron grabs his arm.)
TEEN 1: He's got me!
TEEN 2: I'll help you! *(Teen 2 grabs the carrots and corn and throws them at the Piedron. The vegetables don't stop the Piedron from pulling Teen 1 along behind it.)*
ROBOT: Come with me. Resistance is futile.
TEEN 1: Help! I'm going to die, and I didn't even get to taste an apple.
TEEN 2: Don't worry! I'll get you out of this mess somehow.
(Teen 2 follows the Robot, which is pulling Teen 1 behind him. They move back and forth across the stage as if they're stepping over large rocks and ducking under tree branches.)
ROBOT: Come with me. Resistance is futile.
TEEN 1: Help! Help!
TEEN 2: *(Jumps in front of the Robot)* Aha! I got you!
ROBOT: Come with me. Resistance is futile.
TEEN 1: Watch out!
(Instead of helping his friend, Teen 2 narrowly escapes when the Robot almost grabs him too.)
TEEN 2: That didn't work!
ROBOT: Resistance is futile.
TEEN 2: *(Grabs Teen 1's other arm and pulls)* Aha! I got you!
ROBOT: Resistance is futile. *(The Robot continues moving forward with Teen 1 in tow.)*
TEEN 1: Ow! Ow! You're hurting me. Stop!
TEEN 2: I'm saving you!
TEEN 1: No, you're stretching me in half.
TEEN 2: I can get you out of here.
TEEN 1: Not like this you can't.
TEEN 2: What should I do?
TEEN 1: Save yourself. There's no hope for me now.
TEEN 2: No! *(Pulls harder)*
ROBOT: Resistance is futile.
TEEN 1: Ow! Resistance is futile.
TEEN 2: There has to be some way—
TEEN 1: Let go!
TEEN 2: No!
(Teen 1 lets go.)
TEEN 1: I'm a goner. Save yourself.
TEEN 2: Just because that didn't work—
TEEN 1: That didn't work, and nothing will. Get out of here while you still can.

(The Robot pulls Teen 1 offstage. Teen 2 remains onstage.)

TEEN 2: What am I going to do? I can't blast off in the spaceship and leave my friend behind, but I don't know how to save him. (Prays) God, I know the world is often a dangerous place. Please help my friend and me. Your trustworthiness has no limits. I know I'm secure when I trust in you. Please help me know what to do. Amen.

(Teen looks around and scratches his head as if he's thinking.)

TEEN 2: There's only one thing to do. I'm going to follow them until God gives me an opportunity to save my friend.

Voyage 2: Part 2

CAST: Teen 1, Teen 2, Robot
PROPS: Table, 2 chairs, 2 pies, boxes, gray paint, 2 forks
SET-UP: Place a table and two chairs onstage. Two pies will be needed offstage. Note: Whipped cream in a pie tin resembles a real pie.
SCENE: The Piedron pulls Teen 1 onstage.

ROBOT: Resistance is futile. Sit.
TEEN 1: I won't—

(Pushes Teen 1 down into a chair.)

ROBOT: Resistance is futile.
TEEN 1: I'm sitting, but I'm not staying. Hey, what's happening? I can't stand up. I'm stuck here. I can't get out of this chair, and the chair is stuck to the floor. Help! Help!
ROBOT: Stay here. I will return.

(The Robot exits. Teen 2 creeps onstage in an army crawl, with his body flat on the ground and only his arms pulling him forward.)

TEEN 2: Psst! Psst!
TEEN 1: *(Notices his friend)* What're you doing here?
TEEN 2: Looking for an opportunity to rescue you.
TEEN 1: I've already told you—
TEEN 2: Shh! Here it comes.

(The Robot returns with a pie and sets the pie on the table in front of Teen 1.)

ROBOT: Eat.
TEEN 1: What's this?
ROBOT: Apple pie.
TEEN 1: It looks like apple pie.
TEEN 2: *(Loud whisper)* Don't eat it!
ROBOT: Eat.

(The Robot hands Teen 1 a fork and exits.)

TEEN 1: It smells like apple pie.
TEEN 2: It's a trick.
TEEN 1: I think it's an apple pie.
TEEN 2: Don't fall for it.
TEEN 1: *(Takes fork)* I'm so hungry.

(The Robot returns with a second pie that he sets by the second chair.)

TEEN 2: Stop!

(Teen 1 takes a bite.)

TEEN 1: It's really, really good.
ROBOT: Eat. *(It sets a fork by the second pie.)*

TEEN 2: That looks like a vegetable pie.

TEEN 1: This is the best apple pie I've ever tasted in my whole life.

TEEN 2: That smells like a vegetable pie. *(Teen 2 lunges for the table and takes a bite.)*

ROBOT: My pies are irresistible.

TEEN 2: This is the best vegetable pie I've ever eaten. Who are you?

ROBOT: I am a Piedron. I make pies.

TEEN 1: You're like a baker? Then why've you been chasing us?

ROBOT: I am programmed to make pies. You are programmed to eat.

TEEN 2: I get it. You can help us by giving us food.

TEEN 1: And we can help you by eating the food you make.

ROBOT: That is correct.

TEEN 2: This is great! I trusted God to save my friend, and he not only saved my friend but gave us the best food we've ever eaten!

TEEN 1: Will you come with us in our travels?

ROBOT: Yes. Hurrah! God is amazing. He can be trusted.

TEEN 2: We can trust God to always take care of us. Now let's get back to the ship. We have a lot of places left to explore.

ROBOT: And I have many pies to make.

Voyage 3: Part 1

CAST: Teen 1, Teen 2, Robot
PROPS: boxes, silver paint, stick, 2 chairs, steering wheel, microphone, spaceship
SET-UP: Create a steering wheel out of cardboard.
SCENE: Teen 1 holds a stick. Teen 2 is sitting in a chair driving the spaceship with a steering wheel.

TEEN 1: It's broken.
TEEN 2: I told you a combobulator wouldn't last forever, no matter what the salesperson told you.
TEEN 1: But he said that *this* combobulator was unique. He said its power would last forever.
TEEN 2: It only lasted two weeks. You better change its batteries.
TEEN 1: But it's not supposed to use batteries.
TEEN 2: You can put in new batteries, or you can throw it away.
TEEN 1: Fine. What a rip off. I paid a lot for this.
TEEN 2: You put your faith in that salesperson, but you shouldn't have.
TEEN 1: I know. I know. You told me that at the time. *(Throws down the stick.)* That's it. I won't believe anything or anyone has limitless power again.
TEEN 2: Don't go too far.
TEEN 1: I'm not. I've learned my lesson. Nothing goes on forever.
TEEN 2: What about outer space?
TEEN 1: It doesn't go on forever. Nothing does.
TEEN 2: God and his power go on forever.
TEEN 1: They only go to the end of our sector.
TEEN 2: God's power has no limits.

(Robot enters and slowly moves toward them. His movements are stiff and mechanical. His words are pronounced individually, like those found on an answering machine.)

ROBOT: Ready to eat?
TEEN 1: We just finished eating.
ROBOT: There are more pies to eat.
TEEN 1: Your ability to make pies has no limits.
ROBOT: Funny. My pies run out when I have no ingredients.
TEEN 2: So you don't think that God's power goes beyond our sector?
TEEN 1: No. God's power runs out wherever our sector runs out.
TEEN 2: God's power doesn't run out.
TEEN 1: Does too.
TEEN 2: Does not.
ROBOT: Let's find out. I've got food.

TEEN 2: We're heading to the end of this sector. This should show you that you can put your faith in God because his power has no limits. Hold on. *(Everyone onstage leans to the left, then back, then to the right, and then back again to mimic how their spaceship is traveling.)*

TEEN 1: We're at the end of our sector.

TEEN 2: God's power is still here.

TEEN 1: Look *(Points ahead as if outside of the window).* There are other sectors.

(All characters lean forward as if looking out of the window.)

ROBOT: God is powerful.

TEEN 2: Let's go to the end of this solar system.

TEEN 1: Step on it.

(Everyone onstage leans back as if they're going fast.)

ROBOT: What is ahead of us?

TEEN 1: It looks like a lot of dark blobs.

TEEN 2: Oh no! It's an asteroid field.

(Everyone onstage leans to the left, then to the right, then to the left, and then back again to mimic the movements of their spaceship.)

TEEN 1: Phew! We barely made it through.

TEEN 2: And we're approaching the end of our solar system.

ROBOT: There it went. We passed it.

TEEN 1: Our solar system may be gone, but look; there're a lot of others out there.

TEEN 2: Straight ahead! We're headed to the end of the galaxy.

(Everyone onstage leans back as if they're going fast.)

ROBOT: What is ahead of us?

TEEN 1: It looks like something enormous.

TEEN 2: Oh no! It's a rock. It's so big it seems to go on forever.

(Everyone onstage leans to the left, then back, then down, then to the right, and then back again to mimic traveling in the spaceship.) We can't go over it.

TEEN 1: Can't go under it.

ROBOT: Cannot go around it.

TEEN 2: What is it?

TEEN 1: It's the end of the galaxy.

TEEN 2: No.

TEEN 1: Yeah. The galaxy stops here. There's nowhere else to go.

ROBOT: Apple pie, anyone?

TEEN 1: Not now, Piedron.

TEEN 2: I can't believe we're here.

TEEN 1: The end of the galaxy.

ROBOT: There is no more.

TEEN 2: On the other side of this rock wall, there is nothing.

TEEN 1: I didn't think there would be a wall at the end of the galaxy. I don't know what I expected, but it wasn't a rock wall.

ROBOT: Walls keep people safe.

TEEN 2: I guess it does keep us from falling off the end of the galaxy.

TEEN 1: God's power ends here.

TEEN 2: No, it doesn't. Look! Is that a cave?

ROBOT: A small cave.

TEEN 1: Too small for our spaceship to go through.

TEEN 2: But it's a cave.

TEEN 1: A dead end cave.

TEEN 2: Maybe.

TEEN 1: You're not going to –

TEEN 2: I have to explore it.

TEEN 1: It's just a cave.

TEEN 2: You might be right, but there's only one way to find out. I'm going to suit up and go out of the spaceship to explore it.

TEEN 1: Why won't you accept what you see in front of you?

TEEN 2: I see an opening. Until I know that opening is a cave, I can't accept it.

TEEN 1: The galaxy ends here. God's power ends here.

TEEN 2: Maybe. *(Stands up, gives Teen 1 the steering wheel, and moves toward offstage.)* **But I doubt it.**

(Teen 2 exits.)

TEEN 2: *(Offstage and over the microphone)* **Can you hear me?**

ROBOT: He is coming in through audio.

TEEN 1: He's going to find the galaxy stops here.

TEEN 2: *(Offstage)* **I'm stepping out of the spaceship and heading toward the cave. I'll make contact again when I get there. Over and out.**

Voyage 3: Part 2

PROPS: boxes, silver paint, stick, 2 chairs, steering wheel, microphone, spaceship
SCENE: Teen 1 is holding the steering wheel. The Robot is sitting in the second chair. Teen 2 is heard offstage through the microphone.

TEEN 2: *(Offstage)* Wow!
TEEN 1: Come in. Where are you?
TEEN 2: *(Offstage)* Unbelievable.
TEEN 1: Was I right? Is it a cave?
TEEN 2: *(Offstage)* 1, 2, 3, 4—
ROBOT: He is counting.
TEEN 1: Maybe he has space fever.
ROBOT: He is in danger.
TEEN 1: Come in. What are you doing? Are you all right? Why are you counting?
TEEN 2: *(Offstage)* I can't count them all.
TEEN 1: Can't count what?
TEEN 2: *(Offstage)* The stars. There're more out there than there are in our galaxy. And the planets. Some of them have more colorful rings around them than Saturn.
TEEN 1: Get back inside. You're in a cave. You're seeing things.
ROBOT: Perhaps he needs more food.
TEEN 2: *(Offstage)* And the suns and all the planets. They're all different colors.
TEEN 1: Listen. We both know that God is trustworthy, creative, and powerful. His power is without limits, but somewhere the galaxy ends. You may not want to admit it, but it's true.
TEEN 2: *(Offstage)* What you say may be true, but what I'm seeing does not mean the galaxy or even the universe doesn't have an end. Instead, it shows me that God is really powerful, even more powerful than I had imagined.
ROBOT: Would a pie help you now?
TEEN 2: *(Offstage)* The cave isn't a cave. It's a tunnel to a whole new galaxy.
TEEN 1: Really?
TEEN 2: *(Offstage)* Yeah. Put our ship on autopilot and come out here. You're going to want to see this.
TEEN 1: I'll be right there. *(Teen 1 gives Robot the steering wheel and exits.)*
ROBOT: *(Looks at steering wheel and audience)* Yahoo. I get to drive. God's power really has no limits.

Voyage 4: Part 1

CAST: Teen 1, Teen 2, Robot

PROPS: blanket, 2 sets of boots, sound of a jet pack (ideas for the sound of a jetpack: an aerosol spray can [like room freshener], a microphone dragged across a carpet square, a compressor-sound of air being released [hi-tech], letting air out of a tire [low-tech], or someone saying, "Psht. Psht." into a microphone offstage), tools (such as a hammer, wrench, and large nails).

SET-UP: A blanket should be set on the ground toward the front of the stage.

SCENE: Teen 1, Teen 2, and Robot are standing on the blanket. Their movements are all in slow motion.

TEEN 1: Graturnium is an amazing planet. There's almost no gravity.

TEEN 2: If it weren't for our weighted boots, we'd be floating away.

(Robot's movements are stiff and mechanical. His words are pronounced individually, like those found on an answering machine. He pronounces individual syllables in long words.)

ROBOT: Boots are good, but I do not need them. My jet blasters keep me here.

(Occasional blasts from a jet pack should be heard throughout this scene. Whenever one goes off, Robot should slightly turn in one direction or another.)

TEEN 1: Watch me do a jumping jack. *(He does exaggerated jumping jacks in slow motion, pretending to jump high. Teen 2 laughs.)*

ROBOT: Very good. Are you hungry after all that exercise?

TEEN 1: *(Laughing)* Not yet. Without gravity, we can do all sorts of fun things.

TEEN 2: Watch me run across this rock. *(Runs in slow motion across the blanket. He should jump high with each running step.)*

ROBOT: Excellent! Hungry?

TEEN 2: No.

TEEN 1: Watch me do a somersault. *(Does a slow motion forward roll and then pops up into a standing position with a jump.)*

ROBOT: That was a definite ten. To keep up your strength, you should eat something.

TEEN 1: I will in a little bit.

TEEN 2: You've got to try this. Running in place is amazing. *(Runs in place in slow motion and jumps up high for each running step.)*

TEEN 1: That looks great. *(Teen 1 runs in place too.)*

ROBOT: Careful.

TEEN 2: Look how high I'm getting. *(Jumps as he runs in place.)*

TEEN 1: I can get higher. *(He jumps as he runs in place.)*

TEEN 2: That wasn't higher. *(They both try to beat each other, but then Teen 1 sits down and yanks off his boots.)* What're you doing?

TEEN 1: They were holding me back. Watch me now. *(Jumps while running in place.)*

TEEN 2: No! Don't do that!

ROBOT: Your boots were the only thing keeping you here. You need your weighted boots.

TEEN 1: I'm so high. I win. *(Slow motion. He moves away from the blanket as if he's floating away.)* Oh no. Help me! I'm floating away. I can't get back. Gravity isn't pulling me back to you.

TEEN 2: What're we going to do?

ROBOT: I will help. *(Uses jet boosters to go off the rock. Whichever way he wants to turn, he uses his opposite booster, but whenever he gets near Teen 1, Teen 1 goes farther from him. The air from the jet boosters have too much force for Robot to draw near.)* It is not working.

TEEN 1: Your jet packs are too strong.

ROBOT: Whenever I get close, he goes farther away.

TEEN 1: Help me!

TEEN 2: I have an idea. Piedron, come here, quickly. *(The Robot goes back to Teen 2 as Teen 1 continues to slowly float farther away.)* Do you still have those tennis balls we found in the tunnel at coordinate 698?

ROBOT: Yes, but how will those help? *(Lands next to Teen 2)*

TEEN 2: No time to explain. We have to hurry!

TEEN 1: Help! Help me!

ROBOT: We will help soon. *(Turns his back to the audience so that Teen 2 can work on his front side. Teen 2 takes tools from his pockets and clanks them together as if he's working on the Robot throughout the following conversation.)*

TEEN 1: I need help now!

ROBOT: Careful. That tickles.

TEEN 1: Throw me my shoes.

TEEN 2: They're too heavy.

TEEN 1: If I keep floating, I'll float into outer space.

TEEN 2: Don't worry. We'll get you back here somehow.

TEEN 1: Do you have a plan?

TEEN 2: I do.

ROBOT: Quit tickling me. *(Makes a mechanical robot laugh.)*

TEEN 1: Hurry! *(Teen 1 floats offstage.)*

TEEN 2: I'm working as fast as I know how.

ROBOT: *(Mechanical robot laughs.)*

TEEN 2: That should do it. *(He puts away his tools.)*

TEEN 1: *(Offstage and faint)* I can't see you.

TEEN 2: We're coming to get you. Don't panic.

TEEN 1: *(Offstage and faint)* That's easy for you to say. You're not the one floating away.

TEEN 2: *(To Robot)* Do you understand what you have to do?

ROBOT: I do.

TEEN 2: Then off you go.

ROBOT: Up, up, and away. I've always wanted to say that. *(The Robot uses his jet pack and flies offstage after Teen 1.)*

TEEN 2: I hope this works.

TEEN 1: Ow! Stop that! That hurts. Help me!

Voyage 4: Part 2

CAST: Teen 1, Teen 2, Robot

PROPS: blanket, 2 sets of boots, tennis balls, tools (such as a hammer, wrench, and large nails), sound of a jet pack (ideas for the sound of a jetpack: an aerosol spray can [like room freshener], a microphone dragged across a carpet square, a compressor-sound of air being released [hi-tech], letting air out of a tire [low-tech], or someone saying, "Psht. Psht." into a microphone offstage).

SET-UP: Teen 2 is standing on the blanket. All movements are in slow motion. Teen 1 appears onstage. Occasionally, a ball from offstage hits him and pushes him toward the rock until he gets there. As the Robot jets himself back, Teen 2 grabs Teen 1 and pulls him onto the rock.

TEEN 1: I made it. Do you know what that Piedron did to me?

TEEN 2: Piedron saved your life.

TEEN 1: No, it didn't. While I was out there, already down on my luck, it threw tennis balls at me. There was nothing I could do about it, and he knew it. *(Teen 1 puts on his boots throughout this scene.)*

TEEN 2: He wasn't shooting tennis balls at you to hurt you.

ROBOT: *(Lands)* No thanks are necessary.

TEEN 1: No thanks will come from me. It didn't save me. It hurt me.

TEEN 2: We don't have gravity here, but we still have physics. Every action requires an equal and opposite reaction.

TEEN 1: Oh, I get it.

ROBOT: It was nothing. I am a hero. Hurrah!

TEEN 2: Every time a ball hit you, it pushed you closer to this rock. Piedron couldn't get near you because of his jet packs, but the balls could. He used them to direct you back here safely.

ROBOT: It was nothing.

TEEN 1: Thanks, Piedron. How did you ever think of that?

ROBOT: I did not think of the plan.

TEEN 2: I did.

TEEN 1: How did you think of it?

TEEN 2: Limits.

TEEN 1: Huh?

TEEN 2: We were no longer limited by gravity, but I thought about our other limitations. Then I used one of those limitations to work for you instead of against you.

TEEN 1: I guess limits can be good.

TEEN 2: They're for us. They show us we're human and not the one in control, like God. Even my plans have limits, but fortunately everything worked out this time.

TEEN 1: You're right. Only God's plan doesn't have any limits.

TEEN 2: His plan is created to draw each one of us to him, no matter what.

TEEN 1: It defies gravity.

TEEN 2: And physics.

ROBOT: And pie baking recipes.

TEEN 1: Wow! Now that's amazing.

TEEN 2: We can live boldly, not afraid of every limit we have, because our God is looking out for us and can do anything he wants to do.

TEEN 1: Hey, Piedron. I'm getting hungry.

ROBOT: Too bad.

TEEN 1: Too bad? What do you mean, too bad? I said I was hungry. Doesn't that make you happy?

TEEN 2: He can't make food right now.

TEEN 1: Why not?

TEEN 2: To save you, I had to change him from a pie-baking machine to a tennis-ball throwing machine.

TEEN 1: Can you change him back?

TEEN 2: Sure, but let's get back to the ship. We've had enough adventures for today.

ROBOT: Wait. Before we go back—

TEEN 2: What is it, Piedron?

ROBOT: Tennis anyone?

Voyage 5: Part 1

CAST: Teen 1, Teen 2, Robot

PROPS: 1 potted plant, 1 identical pot with dirt in it, 2 pies (pie tins filled with whipped cream make great-looking pies)

SCENE: Teen 1, Teen 2, and the Robot are onstage. Teen 1 is holding a pot with dirt in it. The Robot's movements are stiff and mechanical. His words are pronounced individually, like those found on an answering machine.

TEEN 1: You'll never guess where we are.

TEEN 2: Coordinate 897?

TEEN 1: No.

TEEN 2: 368?

TEEN 1: No.

ROBOT: Sector Graviton?

TEEN 1: No

TEEN 2: 243?

TEEN 1: No.

ROBOT: Sector Markos?

TEEN 1: No.

TEEN 2: We give up. Where are we?

TEEN 1: We're on the planet Earth.

TEEN 2: No kidding.

ROBOT: I have heard about planet Earth. People here like pies.

TEEN 2: That's right, Piedron. You'll have a great time here. You can bake pies nonstop. There'll always be people here who want to eat them.

ROBOT: Hurrah!

TEEN 1: Let me set this down. *(Puts pot of dirt down in a prominent place onstage.)* I'll help you pass out your pies.

ROBOT: Hurrah! I'll be right back.
(The Robot goes offstage. Teen 1 and Teen 2 set up a card table.)

TEEN 1: How exciting for Piedron. His whole mission in life is to bake pies for people. Now there are people everywhere. This is the perfect place for Piedron to live.
(The Robot returns with a pie in each hand.)

TEEN 2: Set them here on the table.

ROBOT: *(Sets down the pies)* What do we do now?

TEEN 1: We tell people that the pies are here for them.

TEEN 2: Pies! Get your pies here!

TEEN 1: Free pies!

TEEN 2: Best pies in the universe!

TEEN 1: Don't miss out. Get them now.
ROBOT: Where are all the people?
TEEN 1: They just keep walking by us.
TEEN 2: Maybe we weren't loud enough.
TEEN 2: *(Louder)* Pies! Get your pies here!
TEEN 1: *(Louder)* Free pies!
TEEN 2: *(Louder)* Best pies in the universe!
TEEN 1: *(Louder)* Don't miss out. Get them now.
ROBOT: No one has stopped for a pie. I want to make more pies, but I cannot until we give these pies away. How can we get people to take a pie?
TEEN 1: I don't know. I thought this would be easy.
TEEN 2: It should be easy. We have pies, and people here like eating pies.
ROBOT: Perhaps people have just eaten. We will wait.
TEEN 1: OK.
TEEN 2: But we can keep yelling. Pies! Get your free pies here!
ROBOT: Eat pies. Resistance is futile.
TEEN 1: Irresistible pies!
ROBOT: People will not stop.
TEEN 1: Maybe we need to get their attention. *(Jumps into the air.)* Free pies.
TEEN 2: *(Cartwheels across the stage)* Get your pies here.
TEEN 1: *(Kicking and jumping)* Don't miss out.
TEEN 2: *(Cartwheeling)* Get them now.
ROBOT: No one wants pies.
TEEN 1: That's what's strange. We know they do want pies.
ROBOT: The pies are here.
TEEN 2: So why aren't they taking them?
ROBOT: I do not know.
TEEN 1: Maybe they're too used to buying things.
TEEN 2: There are a lot of stores here.
TEEN 1: That's it. Maybe we should charge $5 or $10 for each pie.
TEEN 2: Then people will know that these pies are valuable.
TEEN 1: I'll go make a sign.
ROBOT: No. No sign.
TEEN 2: How much do you want to charge?
ROBOT: Nothing.
TEEN 1: People won't know that your pies are valuable if you don't make them pay for them.
ROBOT: My pies are a gift. They are for free.
TEEN 1: Are you sure you don't want to charge anything?
ROBOT: I do not want to charge anything.
TEEN 2: Okay, but people may not take your pies then.

TEEN 1: I've got it. Maybe they aren't taking the pies because we're here.

ROBOT: What do you mean?

TEEN 1: Maybe the people want to take your gift, but they have nothing to give in return, so they're embarrassed to take them while we're here.

ROBOT: I see. What should we do?

TEEN 1: I'll make a sign that says the pies are free. Then we can leave and come back later when the pies are gone and bring more.

TEEN 2: That's a great idea. I'll help you make the sign.

ROBOT: I'll make more pies.

(Teen 1, Teen 2, and the Robot exit.)

Voyage 5: Part 2

CAST: Teen 1, Teen 2, Robot

PROPS: 1 plant, 1 identical pot with dirt in it, cardboard, markers, two pies

SET-UP: Make a sign out of cardboard and markers that says, "Free Pies!" It should be placed in front of the table. The pies on the table should be vandalized. Replace the pot of dirt with an identical pot with a plant in it.

SCENE: Teen 1, Teen 2, and the Robot enter.

TEEN 1: Look at that! *(Hurries to the plant in the pot.)*

TEEN 2: It grew!

TEEN 1: I tried to get this plant to grow for years in our spaceship.

ROBOT: Your plant needed sun and water.

TEEN 1: You're right. My plant needed the sun and water to grow just like people need God's Son, Jesus, to grow closer to God.

TEEN 2: *(Turns to pies)* Oh no! It happened again.

ROBOT: I do not understand.

TEEN 2: They've vandalized the pies.

ROBOT: People like pies. Why do they destroy them?

TEEN 1: I don't know. Most people do want pies, but only one or two people have taken them in the last month. The rest of the people will destroy them so no one else can have them.

TEEN 2: You know what that reminds me of?

ROBOT: I do not.

TEEN 2: It reminds me of how God gave his only Son as a gift to all people, and only a few accept that gift.

ROBOT: Why?

TEEN 2: I don't know. When people accept Jesus as the Savior of the world, they're pulled back into a relationship with God. It seems like everyone should take it, just like everyone should take a pie.

ROBOT: Not everything is logical.

TEEN 1: Telling others about Jesus is hard work, just like it's hard work to give out pies.

TEEN 2: But we'll keep doing both.

ROBOT: God's grace is without limits.

TEEN 1: So we'll be patient and keep giving pies and telling people about Jesus until the right people hear the message and are hungry. Are you with me?

ROBOT: I am with you.

TEEN 2: So am I. And we can start right now. Pies. Get your free pies!

TEEN 1: And we'll tell you about an amazing thing that God did for you!

End Notes

[1] "Rings of Saturn Seen in a New Light."
www.space.com/scienceastronomy/solarsystem/saturn_rings_010607.html
Heather Sparks. 11/10/06.

[2] "Earth Vs. Mars: The Two Planets Weigh In."
www.space.com/scienceastronomy/mars_tape_030819.html
Robert Roy Britt. 11/10/06.

[3] "Mars Data Sheet." www.space.com/scienceastronomy/solarsystem/mars-ez.html#Scene_1
NO AUTHOR FOUND. 11/10/06.

[4] "All About the Sun." www.space.com/sun/
NO AUTHOR FOUND. 11/10/06.

[5] "The Sun." www.helios.gsfc.nasa.gov/sun.html
NO AUTHOR FOUND. 11/10/06.

[6] "Sun: Facts & Figures."
www.solarsystem.jpl.nasa.gov/planets/profile.cfm?Object=Sun&Display=Facts&System=Metric
NO AUTHOR FOUND. 11/10/06.

[7] "Solar Data Sheet." www.space.com/scienceastronomy/solarsystem/sun-ez.html
NO AUTHOR FOUND. 11/10/06.

[8] "Ten Things You Should Know About Comets."
www.nasa.gov/audience/forkids/home/CS_Ten_Facts_About_Comets.html
NO AUTHOR FOUND. 11/10/06.

[9] "All About Comets." www.space.com/comets/
NO AUTHOR FOUND. 11/10/06.

[10] "Comets Data Sheet." www.space.com/scienceastronomy/solarsystem/comets-ez.html
ROBERT ROY BRITT. 11/10/06.

[11] "All About Black Holes."
www.space.com/blackholes/
NO AUTHOR FOUND. 11/10/06.

[12] "Black Hole Snacks." www.science.nasa.gov/headlines/y2001/ast05sep_1.htm
NO AUTHOR FOUND. 11/10/06.

[13] "Magnet Fields Nudge Matter Into Black Holes."
www.space.com/scienceastronomy/060621_bhole_magnetic.html
KER THAN. 11/10/06.

[14] "The True Shape of Black Holes."
www.space.com/scienceastronomy/mystery_monday_030901.html
ROBERT ROY BRITT. 11/10/06.

[15] "Journey to the Black Hole."
www.space.com/scienceastronomy/060116_blackhole_journey.html#Scene_1
KER THAN. 11/10/06.